# QUIN
# WOOD
# DIVISION

# QUIN WOOD DIVISION

*The Perpetual Love Story*

OLIVE
OMNIPOTENT

**To order additional copies of this book, contact:**
Xlibris
1-888-795-4274
www.Xlibris.com
Orders@Xlibris.com
703229

# CONTENTS

# Foreword
## By
## Olive Omnipotent

The visions feel good in my head, this is an autobiography of everything with no answers everybody should have an endless autobiography we all have a story tell. If I could win The Nobel Prize or a seat as a World Leader or something, life would take on new meaning, I just need money and then my opportunities will be endless. I've always wanted to be like Jesus, all 40 years so far, always wondering what it would be like to be famous, the most popular person in the whole world; well I want to be known in all The Universes With Dimensions and Beyond, being part of evolution forever with **My Angel**. I've been at war my whole life, with my inner-**Demons** and **Gods**. I am a man, an Obsessive King with an Compulsive Queen, a schizoid, a soldier, an inmate, a pedophile, a rapist, a doctor, a general laborer, I am bi-polar, a drug addict, an alcoholic, a killer, a dreamer, a believer, a stealer, an athlete, a lover, etc. I am everything but I'm missing one thing, Money!! So if I had money, would it make my life rectified and justifiable? It would give me one of the best feelings and change my life completely for the better, justifiable? No!! It would give me karma and I take karma well, deep down inside, my heart will have a smiley face ☺ always saying, it had to come to this? I'm doing this for **My Angel** and **Sons**!! (**I'd sell My Soul for you babe, for money to burn with you**, Rebel Yell, Billy Idol!!) We need World Peace now!!...

# Baptism

## *My Angels wings will carry me on the cross to Heaven!!*

### *Family*

May the bridges I burn light the way, blood makes you related, loyalty makes you family.

I only want **Celestial** at my funeral; **My Angel** is all I need. My mother, my only sister are not on my friends list on Facebook and my sons mother has taken my son away from me and my father killed himself....

*Says something about me eh!!*

*You have....*
### *QuinWoodDivison: The Perpetual Love Story*

Find out about the mind of **Olive Omnipotent** the abnormal way of thinking.

(250 for each *child*, praying to add other *250*) Only *seven hundred & fifty* copies will be signed out of *1,000,000*, with **My Angels** signature, we sign them together now that's loyalty!! Love and understanding is thicker than anything, happily ever after is now once upon a time!!

Flip a *coin* to see which way you read this book from past to present or present to past (if you read it from present to past start from the centre *(Forward Psychology) (Reverse Psychology).* There's a different feeling you get when you read this book in whatever direction.... *It's your choice!! Heads you read it centre to back, front to centre, Tails you continue on!!*

### *Copyright 2013 Olive Omnipotent*

*Made with my iPhone 4S 64GB*
*Edited with Microsoft Word 2007*

**Happy Birthday To Creation**

*July 02/2013 (Hail **Mary**)*

This Book was Created because of Woman and Men and Animals and Everything, with special thanks to ***Honey Celestial Bloom!! Our Angel!!*** With love in all ways....

**Book**
Job

**Chapter**
*Resume*

**Olive Omnipotent**
*69 Heaven Way*
*Suit #7*
*Weedville, Hidden Valley, Faraway*
*G3T G0D*
*112-224-6942*
*Justcallmegod@hi5.fa*

*Highlights Of Qualification*

- Over 20years customer service Experience
- Excellent work record; proven ability to achieve promotions
- Dedicated employee; able to work well in a team or independently
- Self motivator who is dedicated to their tasks and ensure they are completed with high quality and creativeness
- Strong multi-tasking individual who has the ability to remain calm in stressful situations
- Good problem solver with strong organizational skills
- Has experience in several different career fields and I have a wide range of diverse opinions
- Maintains professional relationships by presenting a friendly and positive attitude

*Work Industry Experience*

- Over 2 years in the Canadian Military as an Infantry Soldier; two years of hard work and discipline
- I take pride in maintaining a clean and safe work environment
- Communicates well with customers and ensures that their exceptions are met and exceeded
- Knowledge of chemical and physical adjustments to keep painting products and procedures within guideline specifications
- Experience with a large variety of food preparation ranging from pasta dishes to breakfast cuisines
- Experience with heavy machine operation including Grinders, Punch Presses and CNC Machines
- Skilled and experience including, but not limited to: assembling, analyzing, exploring, opening and finishing
- Turned a 200 paper route into a 500 paper route
- I take pleasure in working, the more we know the more valuable we are

*Other Employment Experience*

*God's Heatreat Ltd.*
Paint Mixer 1995-1999
*Canadian Forces*
Infantry Soldier 1998-2001
*The Faraway Post*
Self Employed – Courier Service 2001-2006
*Trailer's To Heaven*
Order Picker 2001-2003
*Aerospace Machinists*
Maintenance 2003-2004
*Magnets Poles*
Tool and Die (assistant) 2005-2006
*Contractors/Home Renovation*
Construction Laborer 2006-2008
*Unemployed And Homeless*
Employment insurance/ Ontario Works/ODSP
2009-2011

*Hockey Donuts*
Baker 2011-2014

*Education*

*First Aid and CPR Training 1997/2003*
*WHMIS Training 1997/2003*
*Ontario Secondary School Diploma 1998*
*Precision Machining & Tooling 2004*
*Basic and advance Chef 2009*
*Forklift Operator Certification Expiry-06/12/2015*

**Book**
*Food & Water*

**Chapter**
*The Choice*

Everything is food and water, if it isn't we digest it, don't over use your asshole! Shower after you shit, wash away what the body doesn't need. We use moistened cloths for babies and White Petroleum Jelly. When I give oral sex, I clean my lady sucking and swallowing the food. Then we suck each other's mouth, swapping and giving her energy and food (then it's my turn to reach ecstasy).... **My lady** always cums first!! Playing Dracula is yummy (I'd rather eat my wife's blood before Bambi's)

**Book**
*Daily Ritual*

**Chapter**
*Bionic*

*Wake-up, morning, around 6:00am*

- Test ph in urine
- One joint of weed ($5.00)
- One stick of cigarette ($0.30 cents)

- ph strip ($0.13 cents)

Two lemons freshly squeezed with 600ml of water, drink with one multi-vitamin and mineral, one calcium and magnesium pill, one vitamin E pill and one acetylsalicylic acid tablet (aspirin).

- Lemon ($0.50 cents) x 2
- Multi-Vitamin and Mineral ($0.15 cents)
- Calcium and Magnesium pill ($0.10 cents)
- Vitamin E pill (($0.10 cents)
- Aspirin ($0.02)
- Bottle of water ($0.20 cents) x 2

Drink right before 5km run with push-ups and sit-ups.....

After run around 7:30am

300ml of freshly squeezed grapefruit, then prepare shake 15 minutes later, drink shake right away.

- grapefruit ($1.50) x 1.5

**SHAKE**
- 2 egg whites ($0.35 cents) x 2
- 1 ½ cups of soy milk ($0.50 cents)
- 1 banana ($0.75 cents)
- 3 strawberries ($0.10 cents) x 3

**AFTER SHAKE**
- Coffee ($0.40 cents)

*9:00am*

Test ph levels in urine and balance
Just a guide if ph is around 6.0 this combination brings ph to 7.5 plus.....

One teaspoon of baking soda with 3 teaspoons of freshly squeezed lemon, combine ingredients and let fizz, then add 400ml of water and 2 tablespoons of un-pasteurized honey and drink....

-    Baking soda ($0.01 cents)
-    Lemon ($0.13 cents)
-    ph strip ($0.13 cents)
-    Bottle of water ($0.20 cents)
-    Unpasteurized honey, ($0.50 cents) x 2

*10:30am*

350ml of vegetable juice ($1.50)

*Noon 12:00pm (lunch)*

Test ph urine levels and adjust, drink 250ml of prune juice with lunch (no meat) after lunch one joint of weed and one stick of cigarette.

-    Prune juice ($1.50)
-    One joint of weed ($5.00)
-    One stick of cigarette ($0.30)
-    Lunch ($8.00)
-    ph strip ($0.13 cents)

2:00pm

-    500ml Chocolate Milk ($1.50)

*4:00pm to 9:00pm*

Test ph in urine around 4:00pm

-    3 tall cans of Miller Genuine Draft Beer
-    2 joints of weed
-    2 sticks of cigarette
-    bottle of water ($0.20 cents) x 2

Dinner meat included (chicken, beef, pork and fish) with a glass of red wine

- 2 joints of weed ($5.00) x 2
- 2 sticks of cigarette ($0.30 cents)
- 3 tall cans of beer ($2.40) x 3
- 1 glass of red wine ($3.00)
- Dinner ($15.00)
- ph strip ($0.13 cents)

*Before bed*

Test ph in urine and balance

300ml of cranberry juice and then detox tea before bed.

- Cranberry juice ($1.50)
- Tea ($0.60 cents)
- 50ml of Seroquel (free)
- Baking soda ($0.01 cents)
- Lemon ($0.13 cents)
- ph strip ($0.13 cents)

My daily ritual happens almost every day of the year, I haven't figured out my calendar year yet, there will be some fasting days and special meal days. My daily ritual is divided into two categories, Internal and External.... Internal comes out my ass and penis, skin. Taste, nails, shit like that and External is the air and the smoke we breathe, vapours, steam, smell shit like that. With Marijuana comes Tobacco, Weed = Life, Smokes = Death..... with food comes ph balancing, Food & Water = Life, over/under 7.7 = a miserable death.....

- Weed and cigarettes = ($21.20) a day, a month = ($636)
- Food and ph strips = ($51.40) a day, a month = (($1,542)

**Total**
= a day ($72.60)
= a month ($2,133)

Please Help Me!! I need royalties and medical marijuana and food allowance in Canada, Canada's life expectancy is around 85, I want to live past that, forever young. I've smoked pot and cigarettes and drank alcohol my whole life and I'm not about to quit, I've gotten this far and I want to get further with my strict calendar year. I have my own religion and I will go the distance with My Angel, I have Books and Chapters to prove it. Please Help Me get my life dreams of peace and the enjoyment of life in my brain...... Injection once a month and let My Angel and I be free. I don't have Schizophrenia, God gave me everything, now I'm giving it all to My Angel and she's the biggest giver in all the Universes with Dimensions. I'm in a true love story!!

\-    Cook meat separate (including soup)

**Book**
*69*

**Chapter**
*% Holy Grail*

Marijuana = *Mary You Wanna*

Not every son wants to sleep with their mother....

**Book**
*96, The Pill, Miscarriages, Abortions*

**Chapter**
*Two, I don't know*

I lied to everyone trying to protect my sons mother. We were breaking my bail conditions. I also thought WE were pregnant (January 2009) before the NCR assessment. I should have the right to know if my son's mother had an abortion, or if it was a miscarriage or false birth. I found literature in our old bedroom about abortions. Why do women have all the rights? I would have asked her to take care of the child until she gives birth then let me raise the child if we can't do it as a team!! I would have asked because she has all the rights in **Canada!**

*To be continued!!*

**Book**
*Two Of A Kind*

**Chapter**
*Three, Educating the mind and soul*

What if your abortion or miscarriage or child had the cure for HIV or cancer in their soul . (Or even a masturbation) at the same point masturbation got us here, it's life! From the soil (insects) I am not an animal, fish, insect. I can kill them and eat them!!! I'm a Homo Sapien! With **Celestial** Homo Sapiens!!

**Book**
*Mirror*

**Chapter**
*458, AQU Eye Contact*

Make eye contact with everything, learn the soul, feel the soul. Blink, dream the soul!

**Book**
*Three*

**Chapter**
*5, The First Fertilization*

*Have You Heard Of Purgatory?*

Not every Mother or Father gets a pass into **Heaven** (not with this society) we have to make sacrifices. We are human; we have to provide life, to reach the next step!! Only the first growth in the womb, will determine your fate.

*Our family Tree*

*Female **Goddess** (together forever) Male **God**= child (**life**)*

Men can bear as many children with as many virgin wombs on earth as long as he has the first growth, this includes miscarriages and abortions.

This will determine his fate in purgatory. The first child will connect the souls to get to the next step!! Choose one! we are losing the women's soul in purgatory...

I don't want some other man growing life in my home the womb ifs it's pure with my Fathers life!! If it's mine too. It's incest (the deadly sin and only sin)!!!

There are ways around everything, (must give birth to a child and marry them).

Okay so there's Fantasy and Reality put Together = *Society.*

So we can predict our future!! Why?

What if the appendix was the holding sac for sperm? Let say we have a pure son/daughter, let's look at this in a spiritual way (We don't know before or after the first child's growth.. yet!!) say a woman gives a man a blow job and swallows once, otherwise it's incest cant mix... Pure.. Just in case!!

It's only in the natural equations of love, that any reasonable reason can be found. Everybody is the reason we are, we all are the reasons we are. Our minds processes so fast (John Nash, R.I.P. you died with your wife, be with her forever), we can keep up with it. The papers are in the right files upstairs. Jumping from one thing to the, other the web of life. There is so much out there. The answers are here on earth!! The beginnings are here with no end!!

*We have not lost our grip on reality*
*We know what's real and what's in our mind*
*We can rest in peace*
*We will make a difference in **Heaven** or **Hell***
*The more we know the more valuable we are!!*
*Amen!!*

**Book**
*Nest*

**Chapter**
*Smack in the middle, **Purgatory***

1- If you die before your husband or wife you go to ***Purgatory*** (the nest of waiting souls) you wait until your children are married and for your other half, if they die, for the next step?
2- If you don't get married you go to **Hell** to find a soul to break free (find a miscarriage or abortion) the more you know the more valuable you are!! Let's get educated!
3- If you have an abortion (Murder)(Death Penalty is also murder) you go to **Hell** (to serve your time) with the spouse separated (if you find your abortion or one of them, straight to ***Heaven*** for the Solemnities of Soul Mating, child climbs, *The Stairway To **Heaven**,* where they start? The older the higher and that child is on its way to ***Heaven*....** (2 late it's gone) it's a hell of a lot easier to go your separate ways in **Hell** but if you find each other!! Then what's after ***Heaven!!!!***
4- The only way to get a divorced is through an abortion (if you're married and have a child by another person and get an abortion) you and your other half have sacrificed your child and ex-spouse to **Hell**, be happy you're on your way to ***Heaven*** with a fresh start....
5- If your soul isn't taken from ***Purgatory*** you go to **Hell** after the Solemnities of Soul Mating.
6- If your child or one of your children die before they get married, you both go to **Hell**

(Some souls want to stay but they can't we have to free ***Purgatory*** then **Hell** is Next!)

**Book**
*Jukebox*

**Chapter**
*7, Reincarnation (The Stairway To **Heaven**)(Led Zeppelin)*

*(Yeah right roflmfao)*
Humans, animals, fish, insects! We all have the same rights. We are in for a rude awakening. Whatever makes you happy while you're on earth (so its whatever) there are no borders in **Hell** or temples. All for one, one looking for two. If you really what to be an animal, insect or fish, find your better half in **Hell**. Make it to **Heaven** together. Everything is controlled on Earth. Remember we can only produce life with the same species... C'mon people wake-up. So why consume so much flesh and animal milk. We don't need our wisdom teeth and formula and soy milk is better for us (manmade!!)

**Book**
*The Fountain Of Souls*

**Chapter**
*A New Emotion*

There's nothing like a woman's smile. We are losing Mother Earth. Please, Please, Smile. The **Heavens** will open. Give her peace back!!
Imagination is what got us here in the first place. We have never lost it!!
Wherever the energy of life may travel, "mine will connect with yours". When it connects a new creation will mature thought-out and before/after these Universes with Dimensions and even beyond the limits of Space & Time...
Wanting and waiting for your soul to be released into the Unknowing. What's it called? You know after before black matter. There's something else out there.... If there isn't, then don't let us dream it!!

Out of all of our dad's sperm, we were given life and thank **God** for that egg!! Team work!!.. Mother Father (The World), King Queen, Oil Water.. We need to be two!! We are losing Mother Earth our answers to eternal life step two!! The mind (soul) it's endless like the Internet, the black hole of life!!

**Book**
*Incarnated*

**Chapter**
*-47*

If you knew where you are going, how would you change your life?

*More to come...*

**Book**
*0, A New Way Of Life*

**Chapter**
*O, The Newest Period*

*So when....*

*To Be Continued...*

**Book**
*-777, Insomnia*

**Chapter**
*177777771, Movie*

Whoever plays me in a movie, receive two **Gold Cards**. If we die and there's a movie made out of hearsay about me!!!! Those Actors will receive a **Platinum Card**!!

**Book**
*Green 24*

**Chapter**
*Monopoly*

- **Platinum Card** (you own the world you can do whatever the fuck you want with-in reason) if you can prove your blood family, if you're not on the cards list (receive a **Silver Card**)!! You will be taken care of before and after cremation with a card if you're still alive!!!! Promotions are available!! **Gold card** maximum!! (Auditors are everywhere)!!!

**Money Cards**

- **Platinum Card**
$1,000,000,000,000
*Canadian Cash*
- **Gold Card**
$1,000,000,000
*Canadian Cash*
- **Silver Card**
$1,000,000
*Canadian Cash*
- **Bronze Card**
$1,000
*Canadian Cash*
- **Pink Card**
$1
*Canadian Cash*

***Emotion cards***
***Green Cards:***
You are NCR *(Not Criminally Responsible)* and your keeping a secret and reality has made you a walking zombie!!!

*Rules of the **Green Card**:*

Must take the secret/secrets to your grave! Post one on the back of the stone!!!

**Money Card Rules:**

***Platinum Card** = **Freedom***
*(Only bring what you need)*
(Total assets in a country is $100,000,000 *Canadian Cash* over life time ban)
(Must have $100,000 *Canadian Cash* in a bank account in that country no less or lifetime ban)

**Book**
*Planet*

**Chapter**
*Continents*

- *$250,000* cash *Canadian Money* to everyone to start, you can spend it however you want!! See **Book** *One Giant Leap For Mankind (Neil Armstrong)* **Chapter** *Heaven* for your rules if your birthday is before oops after May 2/2016!! Let the games begin. July 31/2013!! Go get your dreams!! Good luck!! Play the game!!
- Canada gets a three, four or five day weekend!!! Use the floating holiday wisely!!! We can make it happen!!
- **Canada** gets a seven dollar bill $7
- **Philippines** gets free health care, welfare, ODSP, pension, no wait, everybody gets it
- If you have over $100,000,000 (August 10,2013) receive One **Gold Card**
- *Pennies, Nickels and Dimes* are obsolete in **Canada**
- If you have over $1,000,000,000 receive *Two* **Gold Cards** (August 10,2013)!!
- Under $100,000,000 (August 10,3013) receive a **Silver Card** for every $10,000,000 up to $100,000,000

- Under $10,000,000 (August 10, 2013) receive a **Bronze Card** for every $1,000,000 up to $10,000,000
- Under $1,000,000 receive a **Pink Card** for every $1000 up to $1,000,000

### Platinum Cards Go To:
- **Celestial Bloom**
- **Michael Bloom-Omnipotent**
- **Ryan Bloom-Omnipotent**
- **Richard Bloom-Omnipotent**
- **Paul Diamonds first child**
- **Little Girl (a daughter we might not ever have)**

### Gold Cards Go To:
- **Olive Omnipotent**
- **Dr. Green (psychiatrist)**
- **Dr. Joints (physician)**
- **Dr. Inhale (dentist)**
- **Jason Shaw (Body Guard #1)**
- **Stan Hudson (Body Guard #2)**
- **Chris Baker (Body Guard #3)**
- **Jason Cox**
- **Joshua Hudson-Omnipotent**
- **Craig Porter**
- **John Derringer**
- **Kim Mitchell**
- **Andy Frost**
- **Al Joynes**
- **John Scholes**
- **Alice Copper**
- **Jeff Woods**
- **Little Stevens**
- **Ryan Parker**
- **Frank Stronach**
- **Victor White**
- **Tommy Davis**
- **William Shatter**
- **Wayne Gretzky**

- **Mick Jaggar**
- **Wayne Brady**
- **Jimmy Carson**
- **Jimmy Page**
- **Robert Plant**
- **Ozzy Osbourne**
- **Tom Cruise**
- **Tom Hanks**
- **Sean Connery**
- **Shawn Henry**
- **Reginald Jackson**
- **Mel Gibson**
- **Sylvester Stallone**
- **Arnold Schwarzenegger**
- **Chris Rock**
- **Thomas Omnipotent**
- **Marshall Mathers III**
- **Aubrey Graham**
- **Ray Edwards**
- **Nigel Leaf**
- **Charles Dean**
- **Adrian Mosley**
- **Daniel John**
- **Dale Chris**
- **William Roberts**
- **Dustin Flames**
- **Arnold James**
- **Kelly Riley**
- **Brian Wade**
- **Ben Glass**
- **Sidney Crosby**
- **Don Cherry**
- **Jackie Chan**
- **Phillip McGraw**
- **Eddie Murphy**
- **Eddie Bauer**
- **Bruno Mars**
- **Monica Wade (lawyer)**

- Jennifer Wesley (case manager)
- Dorothy Omnipotent-Page
- Joanne Wilder
- Maureen Holloway
- Shakira Ripoll
- Jennifer Aniston
- Jennifer Lopez
- Cindy Crawford
- Cindy Margolis
- Samantha Fox
- Tracy Chapman
- Ricki Lake
- Nicki Minaj
- Belinda Stronach
- Robyn Fenty
- Adele Adkins
- Dana Anderson
- Katrina Carter
- Jean Potter
- Tammy Arther
- Cindy Summers
- Alyssa Milano
- Kristian Alfonso
- Orpah Winfrey
- Martina Hingis
- Marry Bloom-Ching
- Nicole Kidman
- Drew Barrymore
- Sandra Bullock
- Janet Jackson
- Janet Gretzky
- Susan Sarandon
- Susan Summers
- Kim Kardashian
- Britney Spears
- Rachelle Smith
- Hannah Omnipotent-Baker

*Silver Cards* **go to:**

**Sarah Omnipotent-Hudson**
**Ashley Omnipotent-Hudson**
**James Johnson**

*Bronze Card* **Go To:**

- **Mexico Citizens generation after generation**
- **David Hudson (if you can get $10,000 Canadian Cash in a bank account receive a *Gold Card*)(*work hard and go get your dreams*)**

*Pink Cards Go To:*

- **American Citizens generation after generation**

*Names on list of cards and new cards* **CAN NOT BE TAKEN OFF!! (I pray I spelt everyone's name right, I apologize if I didn't no disrespect)**

**Book**
*Summary*

**Chapter**
*More rules of the **Money Cards***

**1**-You must give your money away, if you die or the bank owns everything or whatever assets that's not in your will. Excluding the **Platinum Card** (the country owns everything) if you die or go over your max!!!

**Book**
*Generations*

**Chapter**
*Public*

- If you give life to a pure child, that child gets $500,000 *Canadian Cash*. Brother and Sisters get $250,000 *Canadian Cash*. If the second child is the opposite sex from the first child. He/she also receives $500,000 *Canadian Cash*. On their 1st child's birthday!!
- If you have the name Bill, win an extra $10,000 cash *Canadian Money*..
- If You have the name Shakira, win an extra $25,000 cash *Canadian Money*..
- If you have the name **Melaya** Today (July 7/2013) win $1,000,000.75 cash *Canadian Money*. If you have a girl and name the child **Melaya** after the game starts, that child will receive $20,000.75 *Canadian Money* on their 10th birthday, If you have a boy and name that child **Turbo** after the game starts, that child will receive $20,000.50 *Canadian Money* on their 12th birthday any other names will receive $10,000.25 *Canadian Money* on their 15th birthday..
- If you have HIV receive a **Silver Card**
- if you have AIDS receive a **Gold Card**
- if you have herpes two weeks in jail, you have to serve before you know what?
- Murder (eg. Death Penalty) or Rape (eg. Widowed) - 1/2 eternity in **Hell** *(minus one **Hell** day)*
- Cocaine-365 days in jail, Saturdays and Sundays in the hole with Q107 playing on the PA (0.1-1kilo = 1 year)
- LSD-6 months in jail no yard Saturday and Sunday (1 sheet = 1000 = 1-1000 = 6 months)(1-1000 pills = 6 months)(1-10ml = 6 months)
- Crack-9 months in jail no yard, Mondays at noon you will put a piece of crack in a condom up your ass the size of a golf ball until Wednesday at midnight, you are constipated for that time you must give it all back or add 5 years!!! (0.1-golf ball size = 9 months)

- Body Parts ~ you will be compensated, the more important the part, the more you get. If you've lost or are missing any body part or more than one!! For any reason...

e.g.
- Blood (Free)
- Flesh o-oz $1000
- Colon $1,500,000
- Testicle $50
- Breast $1,250,000
- Finger $10,000
- Foot $30,000
- Lung $50,000,000
- Hand $25,000
- Vein 0-1" $250
- Liver $20,500,000
- Trachea $1,000,000
- Heart five **Silver Cards**
- You must pay *Canadian Cash* for body parts if you need them, same price!! If you can get them?
- Magic Mushrooms are legal (Friday Nights from 6:00pm to 11:00pm)(Saturdays 24hrs) take a taxi!
- Marijuana is legal (no driving park the car)
- 16 years old ~ Drive
- 19 years old ~ Drink Alcohol
- 18 years old ~ Smoke Marijuana
- 25 years old ~ Smoke Cigarettes
- 30 years old ~ Magic Mushrooms
- Welfare $1000 a/month *Canadian Cash*
- Disability minimum wage 40hr week *Canadian Cash*
- Pension 65 years old minimum wage 40hr week *Canadian Cash*

**Book**
*Team Work*

**Chapter**
*Caught In The Middle*

I can only teach the teachers!!!! It's a long process, it took 40 years to get this far. My better half is the most powerful woman alive; she has control of my brains!! WHOA finally!! (You Had My Heart And Soul) (Adele) I will never go to family court (what a fucking joke), My Sons Mother got all my rights when I was in jail. I didn't stand a chance. I couldn't defend myself (I can go to one court but not the other, it's whatever!!) She can fucking keep them. Fucking coward!! She needs a biff on the forehead! I've seen my son three times in five years!! The first time I went to jail for it! Its whatever!! I just wanted to hug and kiss my son and see his friends and Tito!!!! I need a third party... Lmao!! Okay Canada raise my son with-out me!! What are you going to do put me in jail or the hospital forever... I will find away!! I will adapt!!! **Celestial** is keeping me alive!! Take **My Angel** away from me and I will wipe you out of *existence*!! My son is one thing **My Wife** is another!!!! You can't control my mind wherever I am! If I have to start over **Hell** will freeze over! If its **Celestial's** decision, I can live with that!! We are in a relationship!!!! All I'm saying is please take care of **Celestial**, we are a team!!!!

**Book**
*6-9, 666666-999999999*

**Chapter**
*69-69, 2ofus4ever69*

Christianity is one of the world's largest religions, with over 2.5 billion adherents, known as Christians. Christians believe **Jesus** is the Son of **God** and the savior of humanity who's coming as Christ or the Messiah was written in the Old Testament.

Judaism generally views **Jesus** as one of a number of false messiahs who have appeared throughout history. Jews believe they are the chosen ones, through ***God!!***

Muslims believe that **God** is one and incomparable and the purpose of existence is to love and serve **God.** Muslims also believe that Islam is the complete and universal version of a primordial faith that was revealed at many times and places before, including through Abraham, Moses and **Jesus**, whom they consider prophets.

Hinduism is often called the "oldest living religion". Hinduism includes a wide spectrum of laws and prescriptions of "daily morality" based on karma, dharma, and societal norms.

Sikhism was not only formed to protect the Hindus, but all living things. A way of life and philosophy well ahead of its time when it was founded over 500 years ago, Sikhism preaches a message of devotion and remembrance of **God** at all times, truthful living, equality of mankind.

The Rastafarian movement is an African-based spiritual ideology that arose in the 1930s in Jamaica. Rastafarians believe Haile Selassie is **God**, and that he will return to Africa and free members of the black community who are living in exile as the result of colonization and the slave trade. Rastafarians accept much of the Bible, although they believe that its message has possibly been corrupted.

To many, Buddhism goes beyond religion and is more of a philosophy or 'way of life'. It is a philosophy because philosophy 'means love of wisdom' and the Buddhist path can be summed up as:

(**1**) to lead a moral life,
(**2**) to be mindful and aware of thoughts and actions, and
(**3**) to develop wisdom and understanding.
*Religion is fascinating!!! We believe everything!!!*

*We are love*
*We are magic*
*We are beauty*
*We are pure*
*We are perfect*
*We are endlessness*
*We are evolving*
*We are mindful*
*We are energy*
*We are vision*

*We are human*
*We are vivid*
*We are walking life*
*We are elusive*
*We are playing*
*We are spirit*
*We are internal*
*We are external*
*We are breathing*
*We are dedicated*
*We are connected*
*We are electric*
*We are radiant*
*We are galactic*
*We are unity*
*We are psychedelic*
*We are infinite*
*We are me*

**Book**
*A True Love Story*

**Chapter**
*777, **Olive and Celestial***

This is real, something extraordinary is possible. That might do us some good. Are you ready for a miracle??

Let's free *Purgatory*, the harmony of existence..

The secret plan was cleverly contrived. These works are the efflorescence of her/his genius!!

Changes everywhere....

You might think your reading the same thing over but you're not!! I will send copies when I feel comfortable.

For instance "I can die in peace" was changed too "We can rest in peace" and "Female goddess (together forever) male = child (life) was changed to "Female **Goddess** (together forever) Male **God** = (child **life**)

My heart is back. **Honey Celestial (My Angel)..** Is still in my life. Good and bad we manage to get through it!! Together Forever.

My last name was **Opportune;** during World War II my Grandfather changed our last name to **Omnipotent,** because there's Jewish blood running though our family. So umm.... I've had a sperm analyst done. I'm seven and the normal guy is 21. I had the test done four or five years ago. Lungs checked. There's a lot that has to be taken care of!! Like, **Celestial**, Me, special family and friends, everyone, everything before this gets started!!

**Celestial** and I will represent Canada with class. Made In **Canada!!** We will never forget the true meaning of love.. I live in the best country in the world. **Canada is #1.** Everything I know, I thank **The Creator** and **Canada!!**

I've served over two years in the reserves, over a year in jail, have had about 45 jobs. My service number is **A51 583 223**, my offender ID number is **1112356245,** my S.I.N. is **894 635 651,** My ODSP member I.D. number is **65824652.** These numbers will follow me the rest of my life in **Canada...** My knowledge of the armed forces, criminal system and total work career, I owe to my hands-on education, I've read one book, my whole life. It was "The Thirteenth Floor" I think I was in grade three all I know is I lived in a co-op in Brampton, Ontario, **Canada.** Until grade nine. My Mom My Lord Hannah let me drop out of high school in grade nine. She was a single mother of two. I can't remember what age but I lived in the co-op my best-friend Tom Stafford growing up. After I finished kicking snow at him from behind and saying some bad things. While we were walking to school. We didn't talk much after that. But if I didn't make my choices that lead me here, we wouldn't be where we are today. Everybody has a best-friend from child hood, Tom would have been mine, we did everything together. I remember drinking my mom's Peach Schnapps and Vodka. We were at my place having a sleep over. I don't know where my mom was, probably with John and Lisa (Toms Parents) or on a date. I knew where she was, I just can't remember. Or doing whatever our parents did, we trusted our parents. I don't remember much about the night. I was showing Tom that I heard we can water down my mom's alcohol and smoke her cigarette butts. Tom didn't drink or smoke, I don't think but he took care of me. I pissed all over the kitchen. I'm pretty sure Tom cleaned it up. We didn't talk much about it after that. We were a great team.

What we did together I did with my son **Michael**. He's my **Jesus!** I took my sons pacifier and bottle away, I toilet trained my son. I taught my son how to ride a bike, I do school projects with my son, I build forts in the woods, igloos in the winter, go on hikes, climb trees and play sports, with my son and his friends. There's a lot I can teach my son, there's a lot he will not get away with too.

Then we moved to Georgetown, Ontario with Chris. Chris is one of the smartest men I know, I've looked up to him my whole life. I remember his car rolling down the hill on the circle at Mondragon Circle in Brampton. He was running after it. He got it just before it crashed into a townhouse but it took down a fence first. I always thought to myself "how do I get as smart as him". We moved without my sister Sarah. My sister was kicked out when she was 14.

I worked two part-time jobs while going to high school in Georgetown, grades weren't the greatest but I passed. I supported my habits. Going to School, Working, Driving, Sex, Smoking, Drinking doing Drugs, Partying, Smoking Weed, had it 95% of the time, (never sold drugs, just hooked my friends up for a high) going to school high everyday meeting my high school girlfriend at school for more highs. There was this church right beside G.D.H.S., (Georgetown District High School) the church opened there door for the teenagers, it was open from periods two to four, most of the time later!! There was a pool table, card tables, TV, VHS player, ping-pong table, fridge, canteen. Getting high drinking skipping class, going to Open Door. Getting sex almost every day, most of the time more than once, I remember having a party, lines in the dining room, knifes in the kitchen, beer, alcohol, weed everywhere, Pink Floyd The Wall on TV in the living room, acid eyes everywhere. My high school girlfriend and I and two other couples went in my room, closed the door turned off the lights and we started to have an intimate moment with the person we were with (NO ONE said switch) the smell, the feelings, the sounds, the visions, the imagination running though our minds, the connection between all of us was out of this world. Having sex six times in one night on acid, booze, weed. Was a work out.

I moved to Georgetown in September grade nine so I should have been in grade eleven, because I failed grade three and dropped out for a year. I started working full-time after I dropped out in grade nine, worked full time packing those white snakes for dyers in the laundry room, in boxes. Got fired for cutting the wire on the automatic tape machine. (I was bored) I cried when I got fired. Went to the washroom for a couple of minutes. Then I walked out, went to the bus stop, then went home. It was my first full-time job.

Then I got this job as a shoe shiner at a golf club in Brampton (good tips). I remember at the golf club, we closed all the doors and windows. In the shoe shine room.

This other guy dropped out of high school the same time I did and we got the job together job hunting. (though school because our moms signed us out of high school because we were under age at 14 or 15) Anyways Paul and I cut all the tips of sulfur off hundreds of matches and put them in a jar, lit one match and threw it in the jar and put the lid back on quickly. The jar started spinning around and the lid blew off and smoke went everywhere and this blue flame came shooting out of the jar (what a kool dragon). We looked at each other and said "what are we going to do?". We kept the room closed up, tried everything to get rid of the smell and smoke, before someone notices and someone did.

The fire department was called, the smoke disappeared before the fire truck came and the smell wasn't that bad. We acted like we knew nothing about it and got away with it!!

My Mom My Lord Hannah moved to Georgetown a month before me, before school started, so I quit the golf club and took a month off and lived in the co-op by myself before the move in September. My Lord Hannah was going from one place to the other, but slept in Georgetown. I know this because I beat Super Mario 3 in a month.

Georgetown was where I was introduced to drugs and alcohol. LSD was my drug of choice in high school, I remember eating it almost every week-end, writing my grade 12 English exam on it, peeking out! (Pink Floyd-The Wall was amazing)(Woodstock also).

My Father Numen Omnipotent and My Lord Hannah got married 1969, they also went to Woodstock, don't eat the brown acid!!!

My high school girlfriend and I broke up, with four credits remaining in grade 12, so I dropped-out.

I lost my license when I was twenty-one for impaired driving. Drinking all day with three buddies and we decided to go to Hooters in Brampton. On our way home, I blacked-out, hopped a curb landed in some guys driveway push their cars forward and took down part of their garage. My buddy said "run" but I tried to get away. Didn't get to far. The cops pulled me over 50ft ahead and charged me with (DUI, driving with no insurance and failure to remain) and put me in the drunk tank for the night. My *Camaro Berlinetta* was a right off!! My buddies hopped a cab back to Georgetown and got caught. They talked to the police at the scene lol!! That's what I heard?

Chris picked me up the next morning and asked me to take him to the scene he said "I wouldn't want to wake up to that".

Then I went back to high school when I was 23 and took a military co-op for four credits, joined the reserves after the co-op (lived off my severance pay from Magna), my Grandfather has pictures with Frank Stronach with $1,000,000 horses

Then My Son **Michael** was conceived in Burlington Ontario, in a hotel room. Born May 2/2000. I had the week-end off in august 1999. I was doing my basic training in Meaford, Ontario. We had the week-end off, before the final test. A 15km rucksack full gear physical training exercise. 15km of discipline, the last 100m a fireman carry over the shoulders, one km each. Grabbing whoever we could get, soldiers were everywhere in front, behind, beside all over. I found a man my size and we made it to the end!!!!

During the summer training, I was a section leader for my room. There was about 10 of us in a section. A soldier was opening his jackknife and stabbed me in the leg, down I went grabbing my leg. Private Shapiro said "oh fuck did I zap you" it felt like an electric shock going through my leg. It took two hours to stitch up. The military was in training for the summer!!!!

After my son was conceived Rachelle and I decided, I should stayed in the reserves and work full-time. Because the training was out east or west for what I wanted to do and we didn't want to relocate. I wanted to use my hands fixing things (full-time)

Being in and out of jail for two years, my longest bid was 8 months. I was in jail for; my record is:

Record (this is what I was charged with, this is what the public can find out, there are ways around everything, if you really want to know my bad side, you can find out?)

**A)** Theft Under $1000
- 1994
Sentence
~1 year probation

**A)** DUI
- 1995
**B)** Driving With-out Insurance
- 1995
**C)** Failure To Remain
- 1995
Sentence
~1 year license suspension
~$500 fine
~$500 fine

**A)** Criminal Harassment
- October 2008
**B)** Mischief Under $5000
- October 2008
**C)** Breach Of Bail
- February 2009
Sentence
~74 days in jail
~40 days in the hospital
~2 year probation
~Banned from Milton

**A)** Breach Of Probation x2
- September 2009
**B)** Breach Of Probation x6
- November 2009
Sentence
~70 days in jail

~110 days in the hospital
~3 year probation

**A)** Breach Of Probation x4
- June 2010
**B)** Death Threats
- September 2010
Sentence
~8 months in jail

**A)** Impaired Driving (drug)
July 2011
**B)** Breach Of Probation x3
July 2011
Sentence
~Charges Withdrawn

We are all here for the same reason, to do our time. You go your way, **My Wife** and **I** will go our way, life's a dirty trick!! What the fuck did we do? Years and years of punishment, murder after murder and incest after incest.

*(Come together right now!!! Life's is nothing but a dream)*

Venting on paper in jail (death threats) I only kill for food, or if they bug me! It's a dog eat dog world. I was charged with Criminal Harassment for; a bunch of text messages, e-mails and voice mails. I have never laid my hands on a woman in a violent way, the messages were about, how could a beautiful family, two people that loved each other so much, that brought life into this world. How could it go so wrong? (85% my fault) I did a lot of bad things to My Sons Mother, if you really want to know, just ask Rachelle, she knows everything!! I Told My Sons Mother..

*In jail;*
　　I was with murders, men that killed their mothers, men that kill their girlfriends, men that killed their daughters, teenager killing their grandfather because he molested children, rapists, some man

tied a 10 year old up to a tree and had anal sex with him, robbers, a man tried to use tranquilizer darts on guards that drive the armored trucks that carry money..... All on my range. I knew nothing about the criminal system back then. The guards asked "do you need protective custody?" I said "yes"! Once you go PC you can't go GP, (I didn't know) if someone passes you, while walking around, working whatever. If someone from GP notices your face around the jail and you're in PC you can't go from Protective Custody to General Population, you could lose your life or get seriously hurt. Inmates should be allowed one cigarettes at yard if you have them smoke them (no smoking inside)(two weeks no yard!) Save and smoke use it as a bid in a game of cards. Have fun!!!

Oh and the hole been there!!! I smoked tobacco and weed in jail, mind you there was a lock down and search done but I got high and had a good night sleep. Until the morning. I lost my job as a server in jail after that, a half ounce of weed was found on another range. A Green judge is a *"Worship"* and a red judge is a *"Your Honour"*

When I was released from jail, I had the shirt on my back and the pants I was wearing with jail shoes. Having the engagement ring in my pocket. I made my way back to Milton, form a shelter in Brampton. I remember sleeping at Rogers Center, covered with brown leaves, for warmth! Pan-handling the next morning at Union Station for my bus ride back to the shelter. I got $300 for the black diamonds in Burlington at a pawn shop. Put it down for a down payment on a car (my money maker). I was charged with impaired driving (drug) again!! (Summer of 2011). I was living in Milton with Joe renting a room from him. I was partying at my sisters, I was drinking but not much, I was snorting Clozapine and Wellbutrin. (Just kidding we need humor when writing a book) Went down to my car for a five hour sleep, woke-up and made my way home. I was pulled over at the first set of lights by the police (3am). The cop shined the flashlight at my face and asked "what is that orange powder around your nose?" I said "it must be Doritos I had some chips before I went to bed I must have rubbed my nose and the residue from the chips must have came off my finger and stuck to my nose". The ambulance was called and they released me!! They still charged me with breaches and the impaired charged. My lawyer got me off. I've been having nothing but problems with cars because of the black diamonds. I had a house, two cars, a pool, wife and son and family pets. I was making close to $70,000 a year working from 3am to 4:30pm Monday to Friday, Saturdays 3am to 10am, Sunday 4am to 9am. For four years. I supported my habits, on my paper route I remember putting beer in snow banks to get them cold, 26er of vodka under my seat, drinking them while I was inserting and putting a rubber band around The Faraway Post, Q107 always on the radio!! so I could throw them from the sidewalk (some papers landed on the roof, always had pot with me!!!!)

Then **Celestial, My Princess**. It was love at first sight for me. As soon as I made eye contact, I knew **Celestial** was the one and I knew if she gave me chance. I would not let her down. We met April 26/2013. I've never had 100% of a woman; I feel I'm almost there with **Celestial**. I treat My Angel like a Lady. She has every right to have to have a fairytale ending. This is real!!

### My Princess

What else could I say about a "Stunning Phoenix"....

She wants true love, doesn't need a father....

She sits there full of life and love, she's still alive....

Is she satisfied, everywhere she looks, she sees wanting eyes....

She needs a magnetic connection, men are trying to reach her, but there's no easy way to find true love....

She doesn't need any more education, with her strikingly attractive mind....

This world is hers for the taking!!!!
**(Queen Celestial)**

(Look at the royal family what a escapade!!
They forgot their roots look what got them there) makes you think eh!!

I always wanted something but never knew that all I ever wanted was more and more of **Celestial!!** I just want to stay by her day and night. Her cute smile and her happy laughter attracted me to her, but her caring loving heart is the reason why I want to spend the rest of my life with **Celestial**. The best feeling I get is when I see her face early morning and when I dream about her by night.

Loving her forever and ever is a dream come true (eternity you and I!!) Her love has changed me so very much. People say I am a different person now but I'm still the same. I guess when you fall in love, everything changes. I will be at peace because I have known My Soul mate and have understood the true meaning of love. There is not enough that I can write about **Celestial,** but I want to end this page by saying that with all my heart and soul and mind, I really, truly, do Love **My Honey!!**
   **(I Love You Celestial XOXO)**

I was baptized Catholic; I'm not a practicing *Catholic*. I really have no religion; I believe **Jesus Christ** died on the cross. I do take communion when I go to a *Catholic* Church.

After My Father Numen Omnipotent Committed Suicide, I think I was three or four, when My Father Numen Omnipotent broke on through to the other side! (The Doors) the rest of my family moved to Bramalea, from Windsor where I was born.

My whole life I finally found what I've been looking for (U2).... I have my high school diploma, I've been to tech college and chef college. I am a *Creationist*. We/they are the only true *Schizophrenics*. I am not violent or malicious. I've been in one fight and Chris's nephew beat me, when I lived in the co-op!!!

*Dedicated to:*
   ***Honey Celestial*** My Universes With Dimensions!! And to every thought that has processed on earth (the brain)... Control the animal population, let's eat in peace!! But most of all to the meaning of life::::: Meat should be expensive, it takes a lot to get to Heaven!!

*Looking back*

**Book**
*3012, Motion*

**Chapter**
*121, Earth*

This will be the last copy for awhile, need to collect my thoughts and view more things. So they make sense... Things are getting straight I trust you all.... Together Forever!!

    Could you imagine if we could move the Earth by the littlest 0.00000000000000000000000000000000001 or the greatest 13112744245678854335577666.0 around everything!! As a team!! We are losing our ozone layer!! (I understand it's the CO2O or whatever in the air that's killing the ozone)

**Book**
*Floating*

**Chapter**
*The Human Body*

**(The Boy Who Could Fly)**

*To be continued....*

**Book**
*?*

**Chapter**
*13, Freedom*

The Meaning Of Life, What a dirty trick, What did we do¿?....let's find out? We've been abused by the *criminal system, family law system and the mental health system!* United we stand, divided we fall!! Hanging **Jesus?** He's tired lay him down let him rest!!! Free **Jesus!!** Then put him back up.. Clean **Jesus!!** Hug, kiss and hold *Jesus* close to the heart!! We love you **Jesus!!**

We Are Ahead By A Century (The Tragically Hip) lets freeze time and make our future!! Everything we do we do for love!!

**Book**
*Unit*

**Chapter**
*Total*

-forever changing, we need answers.

**Book**
*0123456789*

**Chapter**
*XI, Satellites*

The satellites are watching me, so be good when you're around me. They want to be the first to know!! I have no choice our angel holds a **Platinum Card**!!!! I'm good!! Together forever.... We will find away!! Smile **Honey** you're a dream come true!!

**Book**
*32*2'N 31*13'E*

**Chapter**
*Pyramids*

What if the pyramids are a gateway *(teleport)* to other universes *(galaxies)¿?*

**Book**
*Time Travel*

**Chapter**
*2600 BC*

Stonehenge where do we start or is this where we/they come back? We need to chip the human body. I don't go anywhere with-out a body guard (body guards travel ALONE!!!)

**Book**
*One Giant Leap For Mankind (Neil Armstrong)*

**Chapter**
***Heaven***

Must read this on your 16<sup>th</sup> birthday at midnight starts the first day of the month after your birthday, your life will continue after the last day of the month before your birthday!!!! Go get your dreams!! I love you!!!!!! You have $250,000 *Canadian Cash* a gift from **The Higher Power!!!!!!!! CARDS START AT AGE 30!!** It's yours no one can tell you how to spend it but there are rules!!! Thank you for being born!!

1)  Must give $1000 *Canadian Cash* to charity your choice
2)  Must work or perform community service (25 hours a month) until age 25
3)  Must keep at least $100 *Canadian Cash* in the Power Account (cannot make deposits) until age 25 then withdraw the balance and close the account and give it to charity (the balance)
4)  If you don't follow the rules you have to pay it back after you turn 30, you have 20 years to have a balance of $100,000 *Canadian Cash* in the Power Account then give it to charity or spend one year in a NCR facility before age 80!!! Then you get your card if your name is on one of the lists so the faster you get $100,000 or do your time. The earlier you get your card!!

**Book**
*Neighbor*

**Chapter**
*Elevator*

We should go to Mars and have a cumfest (Come Together)(The Beatles)!!! Adam and Eve had to start somewhere.... Earth was planed (oxygen had to be here) we have the technology to build an atmosphere!! The imaginary line, what is it? Every planet has one!!

**Book**
*The Temples Eye And Mind*

**Chapter**
*Curiosity x Infinity*

I was reading "My last name was ***Opportune,*** during World War II my Grandfather changed our last name to ***Omnipotent,*** because there's Jewish blood running though our family. So umm.... I've had a sperm analyst done. I'm seven and the normal guy is 21." I totally slowed down my reading and focused on the letters and movement, knowing what I was reading and thinking and missing My Angel at the same time "that ***Pink Cards*** = 5 **Silver Cards**". Then I realized what I was doing and lost concentration!! It happens with everything, just not with this book!!!!!!!!!!! ***Celestial*** is always on mind with me 24/7!! *Team work!!!!*

**Book**
*Disgrace*

**Chapter**
*666*

-***Olive Omnipotent*** (1 **Hell** day) 1 day = from the time *I* die to the time **Celestial** dies and I want her to live a healthy life on earth being faithful to me with our memories, if we die. There's no *Purgatory* for me (so my soul can't make-love to **Celestial,** until our souls collide and she brings me to **Heaven!!** it's a naughty vision I would have had for the rest of my life!!! Stand beside **Satan**, **The Creator** or **Celestial?** (I will rip you both apart to get to **My Celestial Being**) (*With Medical Marijuana on Earth*)(I'm a *coward* I want to sacrifice **My Angel** first, and then it's off to *la la* land for me with a car, a parking spot, a case of beer, a bag of weed, Baconator with lettuce, tomato, onion, extra Baconator sauce on the side with a poutine and chili cheese nachos, chili and cheese on side and a large coke, with a hose with and a full tank of gas!!) (so in reality today people think One **Hell** Day is longer than an *Earth* Day, so if **Celestial** dies before me, I could make One **Hell** Day, less than an *Earth* Day, the sky could fucking change color man!!)

- If you can serve 25 years 13 hours 15 minutes and 06 seconds or have and still alive in a North American or European Jail receive a **Gold Card**
- If you can go to **Hell** for seven days or more and come back to earth in the same temple receive a **Platinum Card**

**Book**
*Whatever Really*

**Chapter**
*Cannibalism*

Wow yippy I can go out and get a child bring them home, have my way with them, fry them up and eat them. Before **Hell** is gone, its year 2013 add a million years, so let's say I eat someone June 18/973261 so I only have to serve 28751 years minus a second and then be free. Yes and serve my life alone in a cell on Earth with nothing.... No pen, No paper nothing!!!! Omg **hell** no after that I would want to be the one to re-write **Hell**!!!!!!!!! Nope no thanks!! There's ways around everything "say what" boogers, ear wax, toe nails, peach fuzz, skin is food times two if you're married mix and match for different taste. (See **Book** *Food & Water to eat if there's no food....*)

- *Eat one pound of your scabs and get a **Silver Card**, you have 10 years to collect them!!*

**Book**
*Look Out*

**Chapter**
*Auditors*

- Are everywhere $200,000 *Canadian Cash* a year, One Gold Cards on Spot (all expenses paid for, then give it back, if you retire or the card runs out)!!
- Minimum Wage $15.00 *Canadian Cash* an hour
- Skill Trade $30 *Canadian Cash* an hour with papers e.g. Welder, Tool &Die, Millwright, Mechanic, Paralegal, Accountants, Managers etc.
- Doctors $100 *Canadian Cash* an hour
- Lawyers $50 *Canadian Cash* an hour

Royalties are the way to go; I once had someone tell me my book would be good for Psychology classes in Universities. (Psychiatrist $200 *Canadian Cash* an hour) So I Said to My Friend "you're telling me my book will be studied and purchased for generations after generations" He said "YES" I said "sweet".

- See **Gold Card**
- See **Platinum Card**
- See **Silver Card**
- See **Bronze Card**
- See **Pink Card**
- Body Guards can only use cards when they are with me or **Celestial** and our **Three Sons**, when outside *North America* or the *Philippines!!* $500,000 *Canadian Cash* a year *Canadian Cash*, once the balance runs out on the **Gold Card** or you run out, you will be replaced!!!

**Book**
*Recycling*

**Chapter**
*The Human Body*

1-  *Re-Use Body Parts* - valuable ones, we need most of our temple
    and eyes (Two **Gold Cards**, one for each eye)(inheritance after
    your temple is cremated) . You will be compensated whatever
    we can use. Cremating the remaining
2-  See **Book** -25 **Chapter** *Three Public*. This is what happens if you
    don't get married!!! We use your parts.... If we use them!!
    A)  Here's a picture of all the woman that died today. **Celestial**
        if this is your wish, that are not married. Pick the prettiest
        one with your eyes. Everybody has standards, I'm not a bad
        looking man, just cremate me with a woman with the same
        prettiness!!!!
    B)  Choose my clothes and hair style and perfume or the other
        cologne.
    C)  My eyes open, standing, sitting, lying down eyes closed,
        change and clean me once a week if I'm preserved. I want
        people, **Our Angel** to come and see me. With glass in-
        between us I don't care!!!! Take care of **Celestial** and **I** please!!
    D)  Q107 playing on the P.A.

**Book**
*Will*

**Chapter**
*Death*

If **Celestial** and **I** break up, I will not harm myself. I always manage
to pray Sunday most of the times at a *Catholic Church* somewhere.
If we are together and something happens to **Our Angel**. I will
seriously consider killing myself. I will not let **My Wife** die alone, if
**My Pumpkin** passes away before me!!!

All I ask is if I die before **Celestial** preserve my body until **Celestial** dies if **Our Angel** dies, then cremate us together!!!!!!!! **My Son** continuing my work through-out this process!!

It's totally her decision just cremate me with the opposite sex!!!!! Then the **Platinum Card** is carried on, choose a good one **Honey!! Please stay with me forever until you're ready to take me to Heaven. My sperm needs to be the last to ever enter you!! "Condoms" you say, I say "I wouldn't have sex if I were you". I'll buy you a dildo, there are ways around everything.**

## Book
*Get The Papers Started*

## Chapter
*Wendy*

If **Celestial** dies before me, I want to be put down by injection, there's evidence in my literature that proves there might be an *Unknown* and I don't want my wife to go alone!! I need help!!!! I will go to court for this, the longer this takes the longer we are apart!! We need to dream our cremation!!!!

## Book
*Quest*

## Chapter
*I feel safe*

IT CAN/CANNOT HAPPEN TO ANYONE
HOW I VIEW AND LISTEN TO MY WORLD
PREMEDITATED/PERFECTIONIST

This is my paper trail....
There's lettering/numbering/symboling throughout....
It's my turn to say no....
There are the things I've been trying to figure out with my mysterious life....
Religion is a way of life....

I had to find my beliefs and way before I become one....
It's not unusual to see and hear me cry....
I cried writing these....
I cried reading them....
I might cry reading them once more, I might not, that's not the point....
I don't know if I can make eye contact, that's not the point....
I can look at myself in the mirror and say "wow," that's not the point....
If you try to manipulate my better half I will make your life living hell....
It's over, it's all over....
I will not lie down and die, I will survive....
These souls can/cannot change....
May the magnetism be with us....
I can/cannot make this stuff up....
Either way I found my world....
Backspace.... Download manipulated/self-governed restricted/unrestricted trail,,, Spacebar....
In the end was it worth it....
Life gets more exciting with each passing day....

**Book**
*Q107*

**Chapter**
*Worth*

$999,999,999,999.99 *Canadian Cash* divided by 2000 years (nothing is worth more than **My Celestial**) hold on to a 1977 *Canadian Penny*. Bring it with you if you have $999,999,999,999.99. Starts Sunday August 18,2013 12:00pm. Or my signature is worth a *Canadian Penny* and it's *free*. If you can get the cheque before this book is finished? You will get a **Platinum Cards** and your blood family you will be taken care of forever!!!! Generation After Generation!! One owner only!!

**Book**
*This Is Some Of My First Writings*

**Chapter**
*Un-Dated Around Five Years*

*(my file at the North Halton Mental Heath Clinic has the date)*

CORRUPT LOVE
WE TAKE RESPONSIBILITY FOR OUR LIFE
THERE'S A REASON FOR EVERYTHING
THIS IS OUR HEART
IT CAN/CANNOT BE TO LATE TO CONFESS
FINAL COUNTDOWN

Even people on television/radiation can/cannot be studied. Anybody cannot/will/can be replaced but will they rest in peace/R.I.P.. We can/cannot believe why she's/him or he's/her. We hope you had the time/stay of your life. How well do we know our partner... Why is our/mine time more valuable than mine/our. What's one thing life can/cannot live without/with. What is beautiful,,, normal and and and creepy. Why can/will/cannot life win/lose all the time. Why do some temples get cancer/negative. Life can/cannot be sin/sinless. Why is most of the public a honest/fraudulent imitation/phony/realistic. A different half,,, without their gentleman,,, is just an empty space. A lady,,, without their different half,,, is just an empty space. If life can/cannot see/hear it has a soul. Let someone else go to Montreal then they cannot/will/can teach us what they think/know they learned there. We might go down/up we might go up/down. In thus study please do not/do travel without us.

We are our sponsor/soul mate. How can/cannot humans confess their secret creation to someone else without their wife/husband knowing 1st. We can/cannot give our world to anyone else. IT'S GONE!!!... We give it to us. We gave us tainted romance. We gave us honesty. We gave us space in the summers/winters. We gave us our soul. We gave us our blood. We gave us safety/shelter and we let our mothers/fathers go happy/unhappy. Wee share laughter/crying and heartache/joyfulness together so far/near. We made each other we know what's correct/false. Now we are giving yourself/us our life line. Our life line has our optimum schedule, voice our/yours opinion to our life line listen/observe. Start from where ever we/u want, have complete/hunger. Be us/yourself.

Every life that has touched our path. Has made us into the holy grail we will continue/backwards to be. We feel alive/scared that our world wont ignore/accept its liaison. Our #1/number 3 love is us and NAME. Unaware/knowing what the future/past can/cannot give us whatever kind of manipulation/love we want if we put our mind/body to work/rest. But we want to feel 2 worlds become one/three

Life isn't too short we have eternity to spend together. We want to see us every time before we sleep and see each other's smile when we wake. Let's move forward jointly we are the best weave eternally. We are trying so hard to endeavor each other. We are found/lost and incomplete/complete. We want to keep calling us baby and buzzing our number. It takes speed/arrest to change 0.000000 and so on, 1. No one cannot/will/can explain how small/long this number is. It takes time -3-2-10123 and so forth,,, to understand why our sponsor/soul mates life is turning out the way it is. No one can/cannot explain how large/reverse this # could be. Whatever way we want to look/find at this that's not the apex. This can/cannot be translated

--- We/different are best friends we want to experience it all together.
--- Our mothers/fathers are under supervised/general/labor visitation/employment.
--- We/different are going to get our child and spend the night/day with him/her we will drop her/him off at school/unschooled.
--- We/different can/will/cannot promise us anything/something. We will try our best to spend eternity without/with each other.
--- We/different are tired we need to go away and make a bloodline>< family tree = 3,,,6,,,9,,,ect./odd/even/odd/even etc.
--- We/different are not crazy, sick or mentally whatever we/you want to call it.
--- This is our world; no one is going to take it from us again.

--- WE USED love trying to find a fairytale. Now we think we are capable of give our princes/prince a fairytale ending.
--- Baby we need our loving we are each other's sunshine/moonlight
--- One +\-1= English/French or words/blindness or independence/ with or solo/wings. I'm going on with our life with/without us. We are fucking free/two/0. gods dam you.
--- We/different are not perfect there's no I or i in team.
--- subject to change... WE ARE CANADIAN!!!... Happily ever after together...

SHERBERY TIME-
TAKE CARE OF YOUR TEMPLE-
50/50 WIFE/HUSBAND

The first little person created by a man and woman get their souls to make them husband and wife. The first/third/fifth etc. Child doesn't have to choose a soul they are born with two the mothers and father. What if you could choose to commit suicide/die of natural causes. It could be out there if you want it. You have to do it the right way and raise your child/children the right way.
Does half the universe rotate around the sun at the same distance or does the universe rotate into the sun. If the sun went out what would you do??? How does it get its fuel is it from other planets. Do you really want your grand children to be born in the year 1000000?? Numbers can go straight to the sun or reverse to the black hole or we can make or go around the sun. Do not make it leap and try to stop time by making it equal.

NEWTONS FIRST LAW

A body continues to maintain its state of rest or uniform unless acted upon by a external unbalanced force = TODAY'S TIMELINE
INERTIA = Resistance to change reluctance to move or act, hesitant or unwilling SHERBERY TIMELINE

## NEWTONS SECOND LAW

The force on an object is equal to the mass of the object multiplied by its acceleration = north and south poles (no I in team) east and west (no I in team)

## NEWTONS THIRD LAW

To every action there is an equal and opposite reaction = Light coming from the sun, elements going to the sun (fuel). From a certain point in time the closer planets get to the sun the more elements are sucked by the sun. We will never find out if life existed on Mars the elements are gone, it is to close to the sun. There has to be a certain point in time where everything will continue to go around the earth or missing it avoiding it. Or we can continue to have the earth rotate on its core moving closer to the sun until we are extinct. If there is no more food there is one way to survive.
We had to come this far to this point in time. Computers work off numbers. The human brain works off letters, numbers and symbols. Computers can be defeated.

BY: DND CALWOOD

My Psychiatrist asked me what I want and I said *"A Credit Card With No Limit."* (Nickelback)

## Book
*C4-H12*

## Chapter
*Gas*

*Gas August 20/Wednesday/2013, $132.9 (GTA) (greater Toronto area)*

Gasoline doesn't go over a $1.40 *Canadian Liter,* spend one (1) day in **Hell** for everyday you have the price over $1.50 *Canadian Liter.*

Gasoline doesn't go under $1.20 *Canadian Liter,* spend one (1) day in **Heaven** for everyday you have the price under $1.10 *Canadian Liter.*
*Gas December 13/Saturday/2014, $101.9 (GTA) (greater Toronto area)*
*Gas January 1/Thursday/2015, $94.9 (GTA) (greater Toronto area)*
*Gas January 27/Wednesday/2016, $92.9(GTA) (greater Toronto area)*

**IF WE RUN OUT, WE RUN OUT AND IT WILL BE REPLACED!!!
FASTER BECAUSE THEIRS GARBAGE IN THE SOIL**

**Book**
*Spaceship*

**Chapter**
*lasers, bombs, ships*

We need a defense operation!!!!! Not everything is kind; there are two sides to a lot of things!!

There has to be a certain point where we are using just as much oil as the Earth is producing. We need Carbon Monoxide (CO) in the air to make the earth move; we can't see blue at night!!! Could you imagine if Earth was the only planet that could move 360 degrees.

**Book**
*Disposal*

**Chapter**
*Hungry*

Dump the garbage in the volcano's!!! At some point in the future the make-up of oil might be different because of the garbage in the soil!!! What if we use Hawaii!!!! (the exhaust pipe of earth)

**Book**
*Big Hard Son (Indio)*

**Chapter**
*Read*

If something happens to me, Big Yellow Taxi (Joni Mitchell) I need someone to get my son ***Michael*** a copy/copies of my literature.... Please, please, please you will get a 500 Gold Cards!! if you are the one and my son reads this!!!! If my son hasn't read it!!!

**Book**
*Others*

**Chapter**
*Teach*

*August 22/2013 10:46pm*
　　Teach/Educate the over/premature populated planets whatever species we might encounter, we might have to kill!!! We got lucky we might be able to control our problem and save these Universes and bring Dimensions together. One planet at a time. We need Earth to last forever like the temple, we control the animal population. life is a walking hormone that can't stop producing life. The human mind is soooo advanced, we have to calm down now or we will be to over populated that we won't know what to do, but kill and kill and kill to share this world our poor grand children. We need to travel and mark our territory. Picture the year 7000 or 106975 or 4099865 or 2050..... Wooow the visions going through my mind I had to pause and fall in love with my mind for five minutes.... Oh **Celestial** I love you soooo much!! Lets just say if **Celestial** and I didn't come together.... This outcome could have been a millennium away and probably a different one, our population is ahead by century plus, I think? 1000-2000 was the millennium of knowledge. We have to train machines don't let them go too far; if they do bring them back without them life has no meaning!!!! Everything is a pet to the human mind, think about it!! We take care of everything on earth!!! Now the universe, then dimensions!!! We Have **An Outstanding Angel!!!!**

**Book**
*Adam and Eve*

**Chapter**
*Sentence*

What the fuck did they do, to be the ones to start it all, what a premature mind way back then. They never stood a chance at coming to a reasonable reason or did they!!! Wow the punishment of nothing in Heaven or Hell wow what did they do????? They made it to heaven tho maybe!! To be the first humans, makes you think about the other side's eh!!!!!

**Book**
*Holy Shit*

**Chapter**
*Alzheimer's*

What if you were driving on the highway and your memory and sight was wiped out and you had nothing but the inner soul to use. Could you make it to safety? Hell could be like that all you have are your inner senses with-out presence. Alzheimer's having your memory erased on earth then your presence at the gates of Hell.... Fuck I don't know. If I could give you a memory chip, I would, but the best I can do is a Pink Card, go buy one!!!!

**Book**
*Uncharged*

**Chapter**
*Evidence/September 9/2013*

***Charges***

Espionage/Espial/Voyeurism/Dreaming - (July 2008)

- Hiding under a blanket and watching a 10 year old temple change into her bathing suit!!

- Foot moved and hit a box before anything happened!!!

- Caught adjusting pants

*Little Girl See Card List!!!!*

## Manifestation

- What if the temple could get younger? How far would you go back? Could we stop it?

- Spy on the spier had to go undercover to feel the feeler

- Sexual gratification was there, it was not at the top of the list

- The desire of getting caught

- The desire of getting away with it.

- Bin there when I was a kid playing hide and seek

- I was wearing a belt and it was pinching my skin in the prone position adjusted after I got caught. Was not hard a memory is priceless and how you get it is irreplaceable.

## Verdict

*Fuck you **Canada** for keeping it a secret, Thank You!! I Take 100% responsibility!!!*

See **Book** *Disgrace*, **Chapter** *666*

**Book**

*Commitment*

**Chapter**

*My Universes With Dimensions*

1) I promise to work hard my whole life providing for our family
2) I promise to love you and only you
3) I promise to fight for us and I won't let anything stand in our way
4) I promise to give your wants and needs whatever they need and want
5) I promise to give you the time of your life

# LEAF 1 & NOTES

**Book**
*Mutation*

**Chapter**
*About-face*

*September 11/2013 7:02pm*

What if we could go from man to woman or woman to man. Look at me I'm male I should have no estrogen, I have low testosterone. I have small balls really small and one is bigger than the other and I can't have kids, I have low sperm count; so this means I have really low testosterone levels. So I should be gay and I am I choose to be with a woman. I'm more like a woman x 10 for eating acid. Human Woman are the sexiest species out there, we have everything on Earth in this Universe. Dimensions are next!!!!

If you have *Schizophrenia* and have eaten LSD = *Schizomania* = need to escape reality everyday = twice a day!!!! You get Medical Marijuana. **Canada** tested LSD and Cocaine on Mental Heath Patients. That's what I heard and/or seen on television. Or like, it was medication or something.

**Book**
*Electricity*

**Chapter**
*Marette*

*To Be Continued...*

**Book**
*Learning To Use Special Powers*

**Chapter**
*Seed Inside*

So in my literature it says there's an easy way to get into **Heaven**. A male and female temple have a child and that child has to have a child. Bingo you're on your way to **Heaven!!** The **Heavens** are watching, that's the first step, remember their names, look into their eyes feel their soul learn their soul. Become known beings!!

**Book**
*Money*

**Chapter**
*Exchange*

*Thursday September 26/2013AM*

I was watching Mr. Deeds last night and EDTV the other night, for the first times, but anyways, Mr. Deeds has been playing all night on the menu screen and bills fall down the screen hundreds and hundreds, continuously falling. What if the pile was there for the spending. If we do it the right way it could be out there!!!! **Heaven = Freedom** we either have it in us or we don't. It's a feeling that travels with you your whole life. We want to be free!!

Thinking it over, if you're a believer!! Send this to whomever the fuck you want, if you want to be free, if you want change, if you have the power, if you have the magic, if you love **The Creator....** Send this literature, send, send, send!! I've sent it (September 2013 and December 2014) to Q107, The Toronto Star, The Toronto Sun, CBC, CBS, MGM, LA Times, **Prime Minister Steven Harper,** The Liberal Party, NDP Party, My Lawyer, My File, My Angel etc .... Together we can make a difference!!

**RECEIVE A FREE PASS INTO HEAVEN IF YOU CAN GET TWO PEOPLE TO READ THIS LITERATURE!!!! NEVER FORGET THEIR FIRST AND LAST NAMES!!**

If you don't, receive a **Green Card**!!!!

Changes are being made, set us free!!

**Book**
*Rank Chapter (Larry Page, Sergey Brin, web page)*

**Chapter**
*Page Rank*

- just fucking around with my mind!! Hehehe
- What's after/before a page?

A-Brain ~ 38.4%
B-Eyes ~ 3.9%
C-Heart ~ 3.9%
D-Lungs ~ 3.3%
E-Scrotum ~ 8.1%
F-Bone Marrow ~ 34.3%

Blood ~ 1.6%
Soul ~ 0.1%
Veins ~ 1.6%
Skeleton ~ 1.6%
Muscle ~ 1.6%
Clitoris ~ 1.6%

**Book**
*Just Thoughts and Ideas*

**Chapter**
*Reality Check*

*(Never stop using your brain!!)*

I'm so smart I'm a retard!!!!
I'm so good looking I'm ugly!!
I'm so horny I'm a dead fuck!!!!
I'm so pissed I'm happy!!
I'm so broke I'm rich!!!!
I'm so religious I'm supernatural!!
I'm so speechless I'm noisy!!!!
I'm so dead I'm alive!!

**Book**
*Respecting Life*
*(Brothers & Sisters)*

**Chapter**
*Everyday*

During our lifetime we are called to rediscover the pleasure of our faith and to focus on the joy that our relationship with **God** is meant to be. We were created in love by **God** and in return we are called to love **God** and love one another. The call to love one another is universal and is inclusive of all people, from conception until natural death? Many in our world today have lost this sense of respect for life; as believers we understand that we have a moral obligation to protect every person as a child of **God**. Set everyday aside to reflect on the value of life and the inherent dignity of each person. On Earth, there are many direct threats to vulnerable people. These threats to life cannot be ignored; we are called to defend and protect our most vulnerable. We can stand for life by supporting agencies that offer alternatives and cures to these issues, by expressing our desire to mitigate life in order to provide comfort to everybody who are dying and by educating ourselves on the life issues. Our faith is a call to action and love in the name of **God!!** As members of the faithful, enlightened by *Jesus Christ,* let us speak the truth about life and in doing, bring the light on these issues to the world. **God** created the world in which we live and **Gods** love extends to all people. **God** needs every person to search their heart and soul and find out how they can stand for life. The world needs to hear that every person is valuable because they are harmonized as a result of *The Creator!!!!*

**Book**
*From Here To Eternity*

**Chapter**
*Witnessing*

We can see into the future. If we read our visions correctly. That's the thing? There are so many before and after the future!!!!!

My role in killing *Jesus Christ*, My role in the fallowing of *Jesus Christ*. I would turn my back on the world too, we are fucked, never looking back. Look what we do to other human beings. With it the way it is. We haven't proven anything. We need our governments to come to a resolution for mankind!! Canadians are the most spoiled citizens on Earth. Why can't we all be free. We made *Canada,* we are equal, this is the world we live in!! We are all in this together!!

**Book**
*Brain Dead*

**Chapter**
*Serotonin 5-(HT)*

What if? When your brain dies, that's it the end of your story!! Naw I'm still killing myself if my soul mate dies first! *Celestial* is not dying alone. Team work!! Next step!! Dirty, Dirty Trick, I want the knowledge of the mastermind behind the game of life. Who/What made the sperm and egg?

**Book**
*I Won The Lottery*

**Chapter**
*$840,000*

**Canada** just offered me eight hundred and forty thousand dollars over 50 years, that's $1,400 a month with room and board and working at Tim Hortons part-time equaling fourteen hundred dollars a month for 50 years on ODSP. That's age 89 could be more? Or less? I'm retired in **Canada** (I will spell period) RETIRED PERIOD IN **CANADA!!!!** Age **37!!**

I got this great job starting at 14 bucks an hour (40 hour week) on a three month probation (fuck man this probation thing is killing me). With advancements annually and of course after the three months. It's like a trade with no papers working with screw machines. On the afternoon shift from 4:30pm to 1:45am Monday to Thursday. I also work at Tim Hortons part-time as the baker lol baker hehehe (yeah right baker). For $10.25 an hour, averaging 32 hours every two weeks, working Tuesday's and Thursday's mornings from 4:00am to 9:30am and every other Saturday and Sunday from 4:00am to Noon. Starting November after training, I'm still at Timmies, just less hours.

Full Time = around $2000 a month take home
Part Time = around $600 a month take home

So that's twenty six hundred a month times 12 equals $31,200 times 50 years at $14.00 an hour for fifty years, but any ways that equals double trouble equaling I'm *priceless* with **Celestial.......** Working forever would be a dream come true!!

**Book**

*Rent*

**Chapter**

*Mortgage*

$472 subsidized paid by ODSP to Summit Housing....
$800 with **Celestial** every week-end (fucking contracts) with our own master bedroom with an on suite with a tub. Furnished nicely townhouse shared with the two owners. We are on our way to owning a small house or townhouse!! We move in December 1st....

**Book**

*Schizophrenia*

**Chapter**

*Quora*

A state characterized by the coexistence of contradictory or incompatible elements.

I've been waiting for this moment ever since I was released from my rock bottom. Thank **God** for **Celestial** and the world and everything. What's it like to "drop everything" and go to Europe/Asia/explore the World forever? You hear people in movies talk about just dropping everything and running off to see the World. What kind of skills do you need to do it forever? How much money forever? How much planning is really necessary? I've always wondered at the feasibility of such a thing.

**Book**
*Facebook*

**Chapter**
*Social Media*

*(Mark Zuckerberg, Dustin Muskovitz, Eduard Saverin, Chris Hughes)*

Facebook gets pages....

**Book**
*E-mail*

**Chapter**
*Typing*

*(Eric Allman (B.S.'77 EECS. M.S.'80 CS))*

The man who made e-mail go. E-mail gets full novel....

**Book**
*Public*

**Chapter**
*Talking*

Public gets whatever section they can get their hands on, waiting for new ones!!!!

**Book**
*Temple (Oct 23/2013 6:05pm)*

**Chapter**
*Notebook*

What if the male temple has to live longer than the female temple. Soul mates have two children one male and one female; those children have to produce life one/two children male/female. Two family trees = pure tree but a family tree could get scarred with one child.... Then the grandmother passes away first, then the grandfather kills himself *(Bohemian Rhapsody, Queen)*. Why live with-out each other. I don't want to sleep with another woman after **Celestial** I'm finished!! It could turn into legal murder/suicide if the human temple lasts forever. Yeah see the male temple is pure we can't have kids, having a kid puts a scar in the soul/temple. Damaged!! So the male soul/temple can out live the female temple/soul!! We keep getting older before we die. Look at what age we were dying at before Jesus Christ!! We/everything are getting older!!

**Book**
*Card List Continued*

**Chapter**
*Free*

**Celestial** and I are driving around North America for six months!! Three months to Las Vegas, three months home. Then we are off to wherever **Celestial** wants to go for one year, a honeymoon **Our Angel** deserves!! then it's down to business, I've taken the dagger out from my back, now it's time to find out the rest of my mystery and why they missed the bulls eye, giving me what I need to control my emotion disorder caused by **Jesus Christ!!**

**Sunny Freedom** landed on Free World; (just sayin) winner of one of the **Platinum Cards,** this dimension comes around once a year!! October 31 each year!! (**Platinum Card** holders must fulfill and live by the rules and fallow the rules of the **Prodigious Book**) (live like a **God/Goddess** and be a **Goddess/God**)

Names will be added with promotion to the books when we are home on vacation/working our full time jobs (must find a full time 40 hour week job for the other six months we are home doing community service for 40 hours a week if you're *a* **Platinum Card** holder when your home for your six months out of the year)

Everybody is getting something!!!!

Names will be added to the lists forever or until my blood line runs out. For updates and new editions to books, You will have buy **QuinWoodDivision: The Perpetual Love Story.** This could get good if **Celestial** and **I** could travel. Considering my whole life **Canada** has given me a free ride, even my college was paid for by Employment Insurance. Now I don't have to work in **Canada**, I will always get ODSP (*Ontario Disability Support Program*) if I need it!! There are ways around everything!!

**Book**
*Waiting For My Gold Mine To Explode*

**Chapter**
*Detonation*

I give it a couple of years, then I'm stable either way!!

*October 30/2013*

I'm soooo in love with you. We have something special that's hard to find, I cherish every moment of the day with you!! I've never experienced these kind feelings I have for you, I'm happy if you're happy, tomorrow I turn 39. May we have the rest of our life together forever!! I love you with all my heart and soul and mind!!
    *Muahh, Muahh, Muahh* millions of *Muahh* **Celestial!!!**

*October 31/2013*

**Book**
*Thank You*

**Chapter**
*Birthday*

*Happy Halloween!!*

It is thankful people who are happy. There's no one quite like those special friends and no friends quite as special as you. It's the li'l things you do that mean so much to me. Thank you to those who thought of me today on my birthday today was another great day that I can add to the greatest day list. When I was sixteen I blew out all my candles on my ice cream cake from Dairy Queen and wished for the wishes to never stop coming!!!! Looking back, I wouldn't change one day of my life, no one can go back and make a brand new start, anyone can start from now and make a brand new ending to a brand new beginning. Thank God there are so many ways to learn. I've learned from you that I need you in my life!! Every single one of you.

Thank you honey for being there and putting up with me. My wish is to have a happy and healthy relationship with many more years to come with you. Thanks for loving me despite my flaws!! I love you **Celestial**!!

**Book**
*Profit*

**Chapter**
*Currency*

### QuinWoodDivison: The Perpetual Love Story

On sale first copy soon first copy only *$15.95,* (only 1 billion copies printed) **Celestial** and I will continue working for one month after book goes on sale, we will sit back at work and watch the Book go Platinum. Then it's off to Vegas planning our honeymoon for six months, then the first money card edition book will be on sale the first December 1st after honeymoon, whatever we are doing **Celestial** and I will sit back and watch the first Money Card Edition go Platinum. Money card editions will sell for $30!!!! (Only one billion copies printed each of the six months for first year) Money card editions starts the first January 1st after honeymoon. January's edition will be on sale December 1st, May's edition on sale April 1st, July's edition will be on sale June 1st, August's edition will be on sale July 1st, October's edition will be on sale September 1st, December's edition will be on sale November 1st.

*World Population around*
*7,046,000,000*

**1 Platinum Card** (October's edition)

The everything is free card paid by The World. (Do you know how much money will go into the world economy) The we have to work for free Earth. Why can't The World give us a vacation on our vacation anywhere we want to go for our vacation time for working full time in this atmosphere... We have an airline!! We have four seasons sucka!! Who wouldn't want summer, fall, winter and spring. We make it around with our spaceships the automobile just fine. I like running for warmth then saying "holy fuck it's cold out there"" know what I'm saying" and saying "holy fuck it's hot out there" just before jumping into a pool. I don't complain fall and spring. Fall being my favorite season, love the cloths and Halloween. My other most favorite season Spring **My Princess** was born May 24.

1 **Gold Card** (each edition)
100 **Silver Cards** (each edition)
1000 **Bronze Cards** (each edition)
10,000 **Pink Cards** (each edition)

Equals $1,101,010,000, divided by $10 Equals 110,101,000 number of copies sold worldwide (if all the prizes go within 110,101,000, which they won't. Based on 1,000,000,000 copies sold, first year)(so really I only need to sell 110,101,000 copies, 75% of extra money will go toward debt first year, second year prizes go up based on 1,000,000,000 copies sold. Six months out of the year, December, January, May, July, August, October.

30 Dollar break down....

$1,101,010,000 divided by $10 equals 110,101,000 based on 110,101,000 copies sold could be more or less. (prizes go up the more books sold) So if I add another $110,101,000 that's another $10 for publishing costs. I need 1 billion copies for $110,101,000 or less, only one billion copies will be sold. Must have a numbered authentic **QuinWoodDivision: The Perpetual Love Story.** Winning number will be published coved book you open it to see if you're a winner.... It will be fair I promise!! $110,101,000 divided by 2 equals $55,050,500 equals another $5, profit for **Celestial** and I. Now we are up to $25 dollars for the book, add another $55,050,500 that's another $5 for promotions. When we are home/working.

## Book
*Debt*

## Chapter
*Bankrupt*

I'm around $1,274,318,000,999.99 (forever rising) in debt with all the money I have given away. There are 98 people on the *Gold Card List* with two ghost spots. Reserved for David Hudson and his first child (if *Johnny's* a bum the rest of his life after the $1000 is spent the wrong way, welfare is next for no reason. Must achieve promotion before I die, if I die!! The ghost shares will be gifts to My Sons **Michael Bloom-Omnipotent** 0.25% and **Ryan Bloom-Omnipotent** 0.25%, if David doesn't become a man) I'm also trying to buy Q107, 3 people on the Silver Card List, 1 person on the bronze list that has the potential to get a **Gold Card**. All of Mexico and the USA. Everybody with Alzheimer's. To clear my dept, I will give them a piece of my fortune. **QuinWoodDivision: The Perpetual Love Story** *Company.* Will be divided up as fallows:

**QuinWoodDivison: The Perpetual Love Story** will be divided into four!!

25% **Olive Omnipotent**
25% **Celestial Bloom**
25% Q107 (**James Shaw**)
0.25% **Gold Card Members** (100)

Any Card under the Gold Card will be given cash. First payment made with-in six months after first year of Money Editions.

Now my debt is down to $174,318,001,000, (grows forever less) after negotiations are made with Gold Members and Q107, so I have to make one hundred and seventy four billion three hundred and eighteen million one thousand dollars my first year or divided by fifty equals $, so I have to make 4.5 billion dollars a year for the next fifty years. Then I can retire and concentrate on all the new babies that were born in Mexico and The USA with-in the fifty years and the people with Alzheimer's (if you die before you get your money, it will be given to charity of your choice in your will or the country gets it!!)

**Book**
*Corus Entertainment*

**Chapter**
*Music*

I need Q107, that's all I want. New negotiations on the table.

Shares divided into four:

25% **Olive Omnipotent**
25% **Celestial Bloom**
25% Q107 (**James Shaw**)
0.25% **Gold Members** (100)

So that's 25% of Q107 and 25% of **QuinWoodDivisions: The Perpetual Love Story** *Company* & $20,000,000,000 Cash, paid over 20 years at $1,000,000,000 a year.

**Book**
*Destiny (In Your Eyes - Peter Gabriel)*

**Chapter**
*What One*

Do you ever wish you had a second chance to meet someone again for the first time?

If it did happen it would put a dent into the space/time continuum (a new dimension)

Lets put all things aside, it would be like going to **Hell** (déjà vu feeling from **Hell**) maybe that's the feeling in **Hell** bad déjà vu, the chance to make things delusional or like *Heaven* (déjà vu feeling from *Heaven*) maybe that's the feeling in *Heaven* good déjà vu, the chance to make things correct. Either way there's a difference in wishes aversion and sympathy. So lets look at this the first way, meeting the second time for the first time with disgust bad déjà vu (hoping things will be different the second time). The only good thing that can come from this is a Fairytale Ending!! The only bad thing that can come from this death!! Now let's look at this the second way, meeting the second time for the first time with compassion good déjà vu (hoping things will repeat the second time). The only good thing that can come with this is death!! The only bad thing that can come with this is birth!!

*The outcome of this is today's existence!!*

**Book**
*A Sign Is Going To Fall*

**Chapter**
*Careful*

Be safe, we need you!!

**Book**
*Sex Drive (Gowan - A Criminal Mind)*

**Chapter**
*Couple*

*God* told me I have to tell **My Wife**, **My Country** and **My Son**. I choose to tell **These Universes with Dimensions!!** I would rather do my time on Earth for my un-sentenced crimes against my soul mate. If you find a new soul mate, you must tell them your confessions before you meet **The Creator Of Everything!!** They must know, all the soul mates must know your confessions, if you make new confessions you must tell the other/others too!! (To make things right). My Son **Michael** connected Rachelle's and I's souls but I'm killing myself to connect with **Celestial's** soul, Rachelle has had another child by another man. My soul is free!! **Celestial's** soul is free her Son's father had a child that died from a virgin womb. But I have to serve One Hell Day (4 an unpunished crime) before I can get **Celestial's** free soul and our son's have to have children! If I die before **Celestial I WILL BE THE FIRST IN LINE!!** My secrets I'm not taking to my grave. The **Devil** wants me, before my freedom in **Heaven**. Ya see, **Canada** can only charge me for creeping on that little girl, if I commit another criminal sex act. So what's about to come out may put me back in jail, if it comes out? If my soul mate dies before me I will kill myself giving me her soul. The longer this takes the longer we are apart. **Celestial's** and my story could make us millions either way **Celestial** gets half, this story could make a lot of people some money. But either way I have found my destiny!! Jail will be easy if my wife (not on paper but **Celestial** is my wife) will come for visits and we write each other. This injection hasn't changed me. (If you take this medication you will live forever) JAIL CHANGED ME. I just needed someone to believe in me and let me be me (**Celestial** gives me that, satisfaction). I'm different!! I've been hiding in the closet and under blankets looking for my true love. I couldn't hurt a thing. If **Celestial** doesn't want me I will set her soul free and hopefully find another before I die, if I die. I know one year from now it could be the year one billion but one day the human temple will last forever with inner-senses!!

**Book**
*Confessions*

**Chapter**
*Cleansing*

I did it; I've told **Celestial** my deepest and darkest secrets!! The simple life of happiness is fine with me, as long as I'm with **Celestial**. I'm leaving the ending like this. There are ways to find out or show

*Celestial* and I some money (let's divide it up first) before the ending of our story is told. The ending could go so many ways but it's a reality ending!! Page 4 is happening and 5,6,7 and so forth will happen in my life I will work and travel!! ***QuinWoodDivision: The Perpetual Love Story*** is a true story of everything. If you have fallowed our story from the beginning or read it with-out knowing how or why you were chosen to read it. (There's a feeling that travels with special people, unique people, different people there whole life) and (I have a feeling you would buy this book with the ending or beginning whichever way you read it, if I had help publishing, directing, designing and re-writing it, it has the making of something fantastic and special) it's could be a an international best seller and let the world sentence me!! Deep down inside I know it's ***Celestial's*** and I's ticket to the ***American Dream*** and we would be taking a lot of people with us and leaving some people behind (The other side **HarshWood** *Shamelessness*) I have to let it go, I guess other people have, no one has said anything!! whatever happens happens. We have hearts the size of these Universes with Dimensions. That's the power of my love for ***Celestial.*** I will not let my soul mate go alone!! I will go alone if I have too and have a miserable death of the unknown Suicide Earth Death!! Once you're born your dying!!

*Like I said I have never had 100% of a woman!! Cremation (if **Jesus** was talking)*

# LEAF 2 & NOTES

**Book**
*The **Devil** Inside Me: Confidential/Top Secret*

**Chapter**
*Prince Of Darkness*

I'm free **God** Dam It!! (more tears and more and more and more fucking tears I can't see!!)

**Book**
*Consequence*

**Chapter**
*Nervousness*

*December, Friday, 13/2013. early morning after work!!*

**Honey Bunny** it's over, my books are finish. That's my life so far. I just want to thank you, you are the most special person to me. You made me open up tell my side of my life. I've had a fantastic eight months with you. The best eight months of my life. I have everything except money, well we can live a comfortable life on our wages. But well you know what I mean. I've sent this copy to my lawyer and my file and your e-mail. **God** bless us!!

**Book**
**Devil** *Leaves The 6th*

**Chapter**
*Cold*

*(January 6, 2014)*

I'm so sorry Celestial, there is no excuse for what I said to you. (Bedtime - "Go To **Hell**" ☹ I cherish ever moment with you. Good or Bad, life comes with the bad. It's our world and we made it this way!!

There's a Heaven made for you and I. We will go as a new creation. The life I thank **God** for. The two of us eternity!! There's a lot going on right now, we have a little minor setback. That will bring us closer in the end!!

**Canada** and my mother tried to NCR me five years ago. And they lost. I went from the hospital back to jail. To face my charges criminally. It was one of the happiest days of my life. I found myself criminally responsible for my actions. Everything I have done in my life has been pre-meditated. I take responsibility for my life. I don't have *Schizophrenia*, I don't hear voices and see things that are not there, I hear and see you when we meet and talk. I just want my life to be heard as a *Canadian* and I want change. My life has made me into the great man I am now, if it wasn't for my past, I wouldn't be me!!

Now my mother has put a community treatment plan on me. She has no right!! Because I brought some childhood experiences from my childhood from her poor quality parenting from the Co-Op in Brampton at Mondragon circle. The kids were one in the co-op. All the children and parents from that era are all special in different ways, the whole neighborhood, not just the co-op!! Everybody was one.

My life was perfect until the disgraceful, infamous mother said "you're not alright your sending your writings to Q107 and the prime minister, you need the hospital". Who the fuck does she think she is (I just want to get away from her ways)(I don't want her as a substitute decision maker)(I have no respect for her) She won't mind her own business!! Her life is full of lies!! Her soul is dirty!!

Anyways if she leaves me money if she passes away it will be going to charity!! CCAA!!

Anyways I got home from my 16 hour work day, sounds like a lot it's not it's not its only Tuesdays and Thursdays every other week, been doing it for three months now!! Got home at 9:30am, sleeping by 10:30am, getting ready to go to work at 4:00pm. I wake up to three cops pounding at my door around 1:00pm December, 17th . They said "We know you're in there you're not under arrest you've been formed you're going to the hospital".

Yeah see I'm writing an autobiography the conclusion the final **Book** *The* **Devil** *Inside Me: Confidential/Top Secret.* I sent a copy to my lawyer and my Psychiatrist and My Pumpkins e-mail. My mom not knowing about the final book. It's about the other side of me right from childhood!! So my lawyer and my case manager got my mom to form me. When I was in the hospital they let me have my phone so I sent a copy of the final book to My mom, she dynes everything and put me on a community treatment plan for six months..... Guilty if you ask me!! Stupid bitch!!

**Celestial** my **Honey Bunny** stood by me and talked to the doctor and got me out of the hospital in seventeen days. (**Christmas** with **My Angel**) *I love her to death!!*

Now I have to fight for my life again. I can manage my own life thank you!! I'm 39 years old. I have lived life been there done it!! I have a credit card, I have a car, I have an apartment, I have two jobs, I have a life. I have a beautiful better half!! Be jealous!! I don't give a fuck; just leave me the fuck alone!! My life is on paper and these books are only a piece from my history!!

*I love you mom, you're my mom. I need to be free!! God bless everyone!!*

**Book**
*The Fairytale Ending*

**Chapter**
***Cinderella***

*If you have **An Angel**, create a **Heaven** for her!!*

Searching for answers though-out this world, with My Soul mate. There's soooo much out there, with little time!! We are on a suicide mission.

# LEAF 3 & NOTES

**Book**
*Celestial and I's New Life*

**Chapter**
*Possession*

*(December 6ᵗʰ, 2014)*

I'm always trying to connect with you, it's because you are always on my mind. I create expectations for myself for your love. The little and big things you do flow through my mind. Be aware of this and realize that it's okay to possess me with your cultivating beauty. It's the harmony of my recurring fight to give you everything in all the Universes with Dimensions. I respect your feelings and needs. You deserve everything!!

*Rules of possession:*

1) If you only want to love it, it's yours
2) If you fit as a whole, it's yours
3) If no one can take it from you, it's yours
4) If you can sense it all the time, it's yours
5) If it's yours, it must never appear to be mine in any way
6) If your building something, it's all yours
7) If it looks like me, it's yours
8) If it was first sight, it's yours
9) If you play with it and you put it down, it becomes mine
10) If you break it, it's yours
11) If you are lost with-out it, it's yours
12) If you can deprive it of existence, it's yours
13) If you're the manager, it's yours

*I love you with all my heart and soul and mind, be safe, I need you forever and ever!!*

**Book**
*Total Domination*

**Chapter**
*999, Power*

I have a gut feeling of supremacy, I'm quite the looker, you'll find my flirtation is quite balanced, which keeps me concentrated on **My Angel**, you know when two souls collide and join, the command of language is electrified, the sensation of aloneness is radiantly snapped by contact, revealing everything. You see how wrong and ridiculous I'm making myself in your eyes, doesn't this help you want to marry me....

**Book**
*I'm Back*

**Chapter**
*Amazing*

*If I could add up all the money in all the Universes with Dimensions, that's how much you're worth and it's all yours. Your love is priceless!! Be safe, My Angel, I love you with all my heart and soul and mind....*

*To be continued....*

A Sneak Peak Into The Future....

**Next Evolution**

**Novel**
*The Perfect Murder/Suicide*

**Section**
*Will You Marry Me?*

# CONCLUSION

# Expressions
# Of
# Gratitude
# And
# Apologies

# FORWARD PSYCHOLOGY

# REVERSE PSYCHOLOGY

# CONCLUSION

## EXPRESSIONS
## OF
## GRATITUDE
## AND
## APOLOGIES

*To be continued....*

A Sneak Peak Into The Future....

### Next Evolution

**Novel**
*The Perfect Murder/Suicide*

**Section**
*Will You Marry Me?*

**Book**
*I'm Back*

**Chapter**
*Amazing*

*If I could add up all the money in all the Universes with Dimensions, that's how much you're worth and it's all yours. Your love is priceless!! Be safe, My Angel, I love you with all my heart and soul and mind....*

**Book**
*Total Domination*

**Chapter**
*999, Power*

I have a gut feeling of supremacy, I'm quite the looker, you'll find my flirtation is quite balanced, which keeps me concentrated on **My Angel**, you know when two souls collide and join, the command of language is electrified, the sensation of aloneness is radiantly snapped by contact, revealing everything. You see how wrong and ridiculous I'm making myself in your eyes, doesn't this help you want to marry me....

**Book**
*Celestial and I's New Life*

**Chapter**
*Possession*

*(December 6th, 2014)*

I'm always trying to connect with you, it's because you are always on my mind. I create expectations for myself for your love. The little and big things you do flow through my mind. Be aware of this and realize that it's okay to possess me with your cultivating beauty. It's the harmony of my recurring fight to give you everything in all the Universes with Dimensions. I respect your feelings and needs. You deserve everything!!

*Rules of possession:*

**1)** If you only want to love it, it's yours
**2)** If you fit as a whole, it's yours
**3)** If no one can take it from you, it's yours
**4)** If you can sense it all the time, it's yours
**5)** If it's yours, it must never appear to be mine in any way
**6)** If your building something, it's all yours
**7)** If it looks like me, it's yours
**8)** If it was first sight, it's yours
**9)** If you play with it and you put it down, it becomes mine
**10)** If you break it, it's yours
**11)** If you are lost with-out it, it's yours
**12)** If you can deprive it of existence, it's yours
**13)** If you're the manager, it's yours

*I love you with all my heart and soul and mind, I need you forever and ever!!*

# LEAF 3 & NOTES

**Book**
*The Fairytale Ending*

**Chapter**
***Cinderella***

*If you have **An Angel**, create a **Heaven** for her!!*

Searching for answers though-out this world, with My Soul mate. There's soooo much out there, with little time!! We are on a suicide mission.

**Book**
***Devil*** Leaves The 6th

**Chapter**
*Cold*

*(January 6,2014)*

I'm so sorry **Celestial**, there is no excuse for what I said to you. (Bedtime - "Go To **Hell**" ☹ I cherish ever moment with you. Good or Bad, life comes with the bad. It's our world and we made it this way!!

There's a **Heaven** made for you and I. We will go as a new creation. The life I thank **God** for. The two of us eternity!! There's a lot going on right now, we have a little minor setback. That will bring us closer in the end!!

**Canada** and my mother tried to NCR me five years ago. And they lost. I went from the hospital back to jail. To face my charges criminally. It was one of the happiest days of my life. I found myself criminally responsible for my actions. Everything I have done in my life has been pre-meditated. I take responsibility for my life. I don't have *Schizophrenia*, I don't hear voices and see things that are not there, I hear and see you when we meet and talk. I just want my life to be heard as a Canadian and I want change. My life has made me into the great man I am now, if it wasn't for my past, I wouldn't be me!!

Now my mother has put a community treatment plan on me. She has no right!! Because I brought some childhood experiences from my childhood from her poor quality parenting from the

Co-Op in Brampton at Mondragon circle. The kids were one in the co-op. All the children and parents from that era are all special in different ways, the whole neighborhood, not just the co-op!! Everybody was one.

My life was perfect until the disgraceful, infamous mother said "you're not alright your sending your writings to Q107 and the prime minister, you need the hospital". Who the fuck does she think she is (I just want to get away from her ways)(I don't want her as a substitute decision maker)(I have no respect for her) She won't mind her own business!! Her life is full of lies!! Her soul is dirty!!

Anyways if she leaves me money if she passes away it will be going to charity!! CCAA!!

Anyways I got home from my 16 hour work day, sounds like a lot it's not it's not its only Tuesdays and Thursdays every other week, been doing it for three months now!! Got home at 9:30am, sleeping by 10:30am, getting ready to go to work at 4:00pm. I wake up to three cops pounding at my door around 1:00pm December, 17th . They said "We know you're in there you're not under arrest you've been formed you're going to the hospital".

Yeah see I'm writing an autobiography the conclusion the final **Book** *The **Devil** Inside Me: Confidential/Top Secret.* I sent a copy to my lawyer and my Psychiatrist and My Pumpkins e-mail. My mom not knowing about the final book. It's about the other side of me right from childhood!! So my lawyer and my case manager got my mom to form me. When I was in the hospital they let me have my phone so I sent a copy of the final book to My mom, she dynes everything and put me on a community treatment plan for six months..... Guilty if you ask me!! Stupid bitch!!

**Celestial** my **Honey Bunny** stood by me and talked to the doctor and got me out of the hospital in seventeen days. (**Christmas** with **My Angel**) I love her to death!!

Now I have to fight for my life again. I can manage my own life thank you!! I'm 39 years old. I have lived life been there done it!! I have a credit card, I have a car, I have an apartment, I have two jobs, I have a life. I have a beautiful better half!! Be jealous!! I don't give a fuck; just leave me the fuck alone!! My life is on paper and these books are only a piece from my history!!

*I love you mom, your my mom. I need to be free!! God bless everyone!!*

**Book**
*Consequence*

**Chapter**
*Nervousness*

*December, Friday, 13/2013. early morning after work!!*

**Honey Bunny** it's over, my books are finish. That's my life so far. I just want to thank you, you are the most special person to me. You made me open up tell my side of my life. I've had a fantastic eight months with you. The best eight months of my life. I have everything except money; well we can live a comfortable life on our wages. But well you know what I mean. I've sent this copy to my lawyer and my file and your e-mail. God bless us!!

**Book**
The **Devil** *Inside Me: Confidential/Top Secret*

**Chapter**
**Prince Of Darkness**

I'm free **God** Dam It!! (more tears and more and more and more fucking tears I can't see!!)

# LEAF 2 & NOTES

**Book**
*Confessions*

**Chapter**
*Cleansing*

I did it; I've told **Celestial** my deepest and darkest secrets!! The simple life of happiness is fine with me, as long as I'm with **Celestial**. I'm leaving the ending like this. There are ways to find out or show **Celestial** and I some money (let's divide it up first) before the ending of our story is told. The ending could go so many ways but it's a reality ending!! Page 4 is happening and 5,6,7 and so forth will happen in my life I will work and travel!! **QuinWoodDivision: The Perpetual Love Story** is a true story of everything. If you have fallowed our story from the beginning or read it with-out knowing how or why you were chosen to read it. (There's a feeling that travels with special people, unique people, different people there whole life) and (I have a feeling you would buy this book with the ending or beginning whichever way you read it, if I had help publishing, directing, designing and re-writing it, it has the making of something fantastic and special) it's could be a an international best seller and let the world sentence me!! Deep down inside I know it's **Celestial's** and I's ticket to the **American Dream** and we would be taking a lot of people with us and leaving some people behind (The other side **HarshWood** *Shamelessness*) I have to let it go, I guess other people have, no one has said anything!! Whatever happens happens. We have hearts the size of these Universes with Dimensions. That's the power of my love for **Celestial**. I will not let my soul mate go alone!! I will go alone if I have too and have a miserable death of the unknown Suicide Earth Death!! Once you're born your dying!!

*Like I said I have never had 100% of a woman!! Cremation (if **Jesus** was talking)*

**Book**
*Sex Drive (Gowan - A Criminal Mind)*

**Chapter**
*Couple*

*God* told me I have to tell **My Wife**, **My Country** and **My Son**. I choose to tell **These Universes with Dimensions!!** I would rather do my time on Earth for my un-sentenced crimes against my soul mate. If you find a new soul mate, you must tell them your confessions before you meet *The Creator Of Everything!!* They must know, all the soul mates must know your confessions, if you make new confessions you must tell the other/others too!! (To make things right). My Son *Michael* connected Rachelle's and I's souls but I'm killing myself to connect with *Celestial's* soul, Rachelle has had another child by another man. My soul is free!! *Celestial's* soul is free her Son's father had a child that died from a virgin womb. But I have to serve One **Hell** Day (4 an unpunished crime) before I can get *Celestial's* free soul and our son's have to have children! If I die before *Celestial I WILL BE THE FIRST IN LINE!!* My secrets I'm not taking to my grave. The **Devil** wants me, before my freedom in **Heaven**. Ya see, *Canada* can only charge me for creeping on that little girl, if I commit another criminal sex act. So what's about to come out may put me back in jail, if it comes out? If my soul mate dies before me, I will kill myself, giving me her soul. The longer this takes the longer we are apart. *Celestial's* and my story could make us millions either way Celestial gets half, this story could make a lot of people some money. But either way I have found my destiny!! Jail will be easy if my wife (not on paper but **Celestial** is my wife) will come for visits and we write each other. This injection hasn't changed me. (If you take this medication you will live forever) JAIL CHANGED ME. I just needed someone to believe in me and let me be me (**Celestial** gives me that, satisfaction). I'm different!! I've been hiding in the closet and under blankets looking for my true love. I couldn't hurt a thing. If **Celestial** doesn't want me I will set her soul free and hopefully find another before I die, if I die. I know one year from now it could be the year one billion but one day the human temple will last forever with inner-senses!!

**Book**
*A Sign Is Going To Fall*

**Chapter**
*Careful*

Be safe, we need you!!

**Book**
*Destiny (In Your Eyes - Peter Gabriel)*

**Chapter**
*What One*

Do you ever wish you had a second chance to meet someone again for the first time?

If it did happen it would put a dent into the space/time continuum (a new dimension)

Lets put all things aside, it would be like going to **Hell** (déjà vu feeling from **Hell**) maybe that's the feeling in **Hell** bad déjà vu, the chance to make things delusional or like **Heaven** (déjà vu feeling from **Heaven**) maybe that's the feeling in **Heaven** good déjà vu, the chance to make things correct. Either way there's a difference in wishes aversion and sympathy. So let's look at this the first way, meeting the second time for the first time with disgust bad déjà vu (hoping things will be different the second time). The only good thing that can come from this is a Fairytale Ending!! The only bad thing that can come from this death!! Now let's look at this the second way, meeting the second time for the first time with compassion good déjà vu (hoping things will repeat the second time). The only good thing that can come with this is death!! The only bad thing that can come with this is birth!!

*The outcome of this is today's existence!!*

**Book**
*Corus Entertainment*

**Chapter**
*Music*

I need Q107, that's all I want. New negotiations on the table.

Shares divided into four:

25% **Olive Omnipotent**
25% **Celestial Bloom**
25% Q107 (**James Shaw**)
0.25% **Gold Members** (100)

So that's 25% of Q107 and 25% of **QuinWoodDivisions: The Perpetual Love Story** Company & $20,000,000,000 Cash, paid over 20 years at $1,000,000,000 a year.

**Book**
*Debt*

**Chapter**
*Bankrupt*

I'm around $1,274,318,000,999.99 (forever rising) in debt with all the money I have given away. There are 98 people on the **Gold Card** List with two ghost spots. Reserved for David Hudson and his first child (if Johnny's a bum the rest of his life after the $1000 is spent the wrong way, welfare is next for no reason. Must achieve promotion before I die, if I die!! The ghost shares will be gifts to My Sons **Michael Bloom-Omnipotent** 0.25% and **Ryan Bloom-Omnipotent** 0.25%, if David doesn't become a man) I'm also trying to buy Q107, 3 people on the **Silver Card** List, 1 person on the bronze list that has the potential to get a **Gold Card**. All of Mexico and the USA. Everybody with Alzheimer's. To clear my dept, I will give them a piece of my fortune. **QuinWoodDivision: The Perpetual Love Story** Company. Will be divided up as follows:

***QuinWoodDivison: The Perpetual Love Story*** will be divided into four!!

25% **Olive Omnipotent**
25% **Celestial Bloom**
25% Q107 (**James Shaw**)
0.25% **Gold Card Members** (100)

Any Card under the **Gold Card** will be given cash. First payment made with-in six months after first year of Money Editions.

Now my debt is down to $174,318,001,000, (grows forever less) after negotiations are made with Gold Members and Q107, so I have to make one hundred and seventy four billion three hundred and eighteen million one thousand dollars my first year or divided by fifty equals $, so I have to make 4.5 billion dollars a year for the next fifty years. Then I can retire and concentrate on all the new babies that were born in Mexico and The USA with-in the fifty years and the people with Alzheimer's (if you die before you get your money, it will be given to charity of your choice in your will or the country gets it!!)

**Book**
*Profit*

**Chapter**
*Currency*

***QuinWoodDivison: The Perpetual Love Story***

On sale first copy soon first copy only $15.95, (only 1 billion copies printed) **Celestial** and I will continue working for one month after book goes on sale, we will sit back at work and watch the Book go Platinum. Then it's off to Vegas planning our honeymoon for six months, then the first money card edition book will be on sale the first December 1st after honeymoon, whatever we are doing **Celestial** and I will sit back and watch the first Money Card Edition go Platinum. Money card editions will sell for $30!!!! (Only one billion copies printed each of the six months for first year) Money card editions starts the first January 1st after honeymoon. January's edition will be on sale December 1st, May's edition on sale April 1st, July's edition will be on sale June 1st, August's edition will be on sale July 1st, October's edition will be on sale September 1st, December's edition will be on sale November 1st.

*World Population around*
*7,046,000,000*

### 1 **Platinum Card** (October's edition)

The everything is free card paid by The World. (Do you know how much money will go into the world economy) The we have to work for free Earth. Why can't The World give us a vacation on our vacation anywhere we want to go for our vacation time for working full time in this atmosphere... We have an airline!! We have four seasons sucka!! Who wouldn't want summer, fall, winter and spring. We make it around with our spaceships the automobile just fine. I like running for warmth then saying "holy fuck it's cold out there"" know what I'm saying" and saying "holy fuck it's hot out there" just before jumping into a pool. I don't complain fall and spring. Fall being my favorite season, love the cloths and Halloween. My other most favorite season Spring **My Princess** was born May 24.

1 **Gold Card** (each edition)
100 **Silver Cards** (each edition)
1000 **Bronze Cards** (each edition)
10,000 **Pink Cards** (each edition)

Equals $1,101,010,000, divided by $10 Equals 110,101,000 number of copies sold worldwide (if all the prizes go within 110,101,000, which they won't. Based on 1,000,000,000 copies sold, first year)(so really I only need to sell 110,101,000 copies, 75% of extra money will go toward debt first year, second year prizes go up based on 1,000,000,000 copies sold. Six months out of the year, December, January, May, July, August, October.

30 Dollar break down....

$1,101,010,000 divided by $10 equals 110,101,000 based on 110,101,000 copies sold could be more or less. (prizes go up the more books sold) So if I add another $110,101,000 that's another $10 for publishing costs. I need 1 billion copies for $110,101,000 or less, only one billion copies will be sold. Must have a numbered authentic **QuinWoodDivision: The Perpetual Love Story.** Winning number will be published coved book you open it to see if you're a winner.... It will be fair I promise!! $110,101,000 divided by 2 equals $55,050,500 equals another $5, profit for Celestial and I. Now we are up to $25 dollars for the book, add another $55,050,500 that's another $5 for promotions. When we are home/working.

*October 31/2013*

**Book**
*Thank You*

**Chapter**
*Birthday*

*Happy Halloween!!*

It is thankful people who are happy. There's no one quite like those special friends and no friends quite as special as you. It's the li'l things you do that mean so much to me. Thank you to those who thought of me today on my birthday, today was another great day that I can add to the greatest day list. When I was sixteen I blew out all my candles on my ice cream cake from Dairy Queen and wished for the wishes to never stop coming!!!! Looking back, I wouldn't change one day of my life, no one can go back and make a brand new start, anyone can start from now and make a brand new ending to a brand new beginning. Thank **God** there are so many ways to learn. I've learned from you that I need you in my life!! Every single one of you.

Thank you honey for being there and putting up with me. My wish is to have a happy and healthy relationship with many more years to come with you. Thanks for loving me despite my flaws!! I love you **Celestial!!**

**Book**
*Waiting For My Gold Mine To Explode*

**Chapter**
*Detonation*

I give it a couple of years, then I'm stable either way!!

*October 30/2013*

I'm soooo in love with you. We have something special that's hard to find, I cherish every moment of the day with you!! I've never experienced these kind feelings I have for you, I'm happy if you're happy, tomorrow I turn 39. May we have the rest of our life together forever!! I love you with all my heart and soul and mind!!
*Muahh, Muahh, Muahh* millions of *Muahh* **Celestial!!!**

**Book**
*Card List Continued*

**Chapter**
*Free*

**Celestial** and I are driving around North America for six months!! Three months to Las Vegas, three months home. Then we are off to wherever **Celestial** wants to go for one year, a honeymoon **Our Angel** deserves!! then it's down to business, I've taken the dagger out from my back, now it's time to find out the rest of my mystery and why they missed the bulls eye, giving me what I need to control my emotion disorder caused by **Jesus Christ!!**

**Sunny Freedom** landed on Free World; (just sayin) winner of one of the **Platinum Cards**, this dimension comes around once a year!! October 31 each year!! (**Platinum Card** holders must fulfill and live by the rules and fallow the rules of the *Prodigious Book*) (live like a **God/Goddess** and be a **Goddess/God**)

Names will be added with promotion to the books when we are home on vacation/working our full time jobs (must find a full time 40 hour week job for the other six months we are home doing community service for 40 hours a week if you're a **Platinum Card** holder when your home for your six months out of the year)

*Everybody is getting something!!!!*

Names will be added to the lists forever or until my blood line runs out. For updates and new editions to books, You will have buy **QuinWoodDivision: The Perpetual Love Story**. This could get good if **Celestial** and **I** could travel. Considering my whole life **Canada** has given me a free ride, even my college was paid for by Employment Insurance. Now I don't have to work in **Canada**, I will always get ODSP *(Ontario Disability Support Program)* if I need it!! There are ways around everything!!

**Book**
*Temple (Oct 23/2013 6:05pm)*

**Chapter**
*Notebook*

What if the male temple has to live longer than the female temple. Soul mates have two children one male and one female; those children have to produce life one/two children male/female. Two family trees = pure tree but a family tree could get scarred with one child.... Then the grandmother passes away first, then the grandfather kills himself (Bohemian Rhapsody, Queen). Why live with-out each other. I don't want to sleep with another woman after Celestial I'm finished!! It could turn into legal murder/suicide if the human temple lasts forever. Yeah see the male temple is pure we can't have kids, having a kid puts a scar in the soul/temple. Damaged!! So the male soul/temple can out live the female temple/soul!! We keep getting older before we die. Look at what age we were dying at before **Jesus Christ!!** We/everything are getting older!!

**Book**
*Public*

**Chapter**
*Talking*

Public gets whatever section they can get their hands on, waiting for new ones!!!!

**Book**
*E-mail*

**Chapter**
*Typing*

(Eric Allman (B.S.'77 EECS. M.S.'80 CS))

The man who made e-mail go. E-mail gets full novel....

**Book**
*Facebook*

**Chapter**
*Social Media*

(Mark Zuckerberg, Dustin Muskovitz, Eduard Saverin, Chris Hughes)

Facebook gets pages....

**Book**
*Schizophrenia*

**Chapter**
*Quora*

A state characterized by the coexistence of contradictory or incompatible elements.

I've been waiting for this moment ever since I was released from my rock bottom. Thank **God** for **Celestial** and the world and everything. What's it like to "drop everything" and go to Europe/Asia/explore The World forever? You hear people in movies talk about just dropping everything and running off to see the World. What kind of skills do you need to do it forever? How much money forever? How much planning is really necessary? I've always wondered at the feasibility of such a thing.

**Book**
*Rent*

**Chapter**
*Mortgage*

$472 subsidized paid by ODSP to Summit Housing....

$800 with **Celestial** every week-end (fucking contracts) with our own master bedroom with an on suite with a tub. Furnished nicely townhouse shared with the two owners. We are on our way to owning a small house or townhouse!! We move in December 1st....

**Book**
*I Won The Lottery*

**Chapter**
*$840,000*

**Canada** just offered me eight hundred and forty thousand dollars over 50 years, that's $1,400 a month with room and board and working at Tim Hortons part-time equaling fourteen hundred dollars a month for 50 years on ODSP. That's age 89 could be more? Or less? I'm retired in **Canada** *(I will spell period) RETIRED PERIOD IN* **CANADA!!!!** *Age 37!!*

I got this great job starting at 14 bucks an hour (40 hour week) on a three month probation (fuck man this probation thing is killing me). With advancements annually and of course after the three months. It's like a trade with no papers working with screw machines. On the afternoon shift from 4:30pm to 1:45am Monday to Thursday. I also work at Tim Hortons part-time as the baker lol baker hehehe (yeah right baker). For $10.25 an hour, averaging 32 hours every two weeks, working Tuesday's and Thursday's mornings from 4:00am to 9:30am and every other Saturday and Sunday from 4:00am to Noon. Starting November after training, I'm still at Timmies, just less hours.

Full Time = around $2000 a month take home
Part Time = around $600 a month take home

So that's twenty six hundred a month times 12 equals $31,200 times 50 years at $14.00 an hour for fifty years, but any ways that equals double trouble equaling I'm *priceless* with **Celestial.......** Working forever would be a dream come true!!

**Book**
*Brain Dead*

**Chapter**
*Serotonin 5-(HT)*

What if? When your brain dies, that's it the end of your story!! Naw I'm still killing myself if my soul mate dies first! **Celestial** is not dying alone. Team work!! Next step!! Dirty, Dirty Trick, I want the knowledge of the mastermind behind the game of life. Who/What made the sperm and egg?

**Book**
*From Here To Eternity*

**Chapter**
*Witnessing*

We can see into the future. If we read our visions correctly. That's the thing? There are so many before and after the future!!!!!

My role in killing **Jesus Christ**, My role in the fallowing of **Jesus Christ**. I would turn my back on the world too, we are fucked, never looking back. look what we do to other human beings. With it the way it is. We haven't proven anything. We need our governments to come to a resolution for mankind!! Canadians are the most spoiled citizens on earth. Why can't we all be free. We made **Canada,** we are equal, this is the world we live in!! We are all in this together!!

**Book**
*Respecting Life*
*(Brothers & Sisters)*

**Chapter**
*Everyday*

During our lifetime we are called to rediscover the pleasure of our faith and to focus on the joy
that our relationship with **God** is meant to be. We were created in love by **God** and in return we are called to love **God** and love one another. The call to love one another is universal and is inclusive of all people, from conception until natural death? Many in our world today have lost this sense of respect for life; as believers we understand that we have a moral obligation to protect every person as a child of **God**. Set everyday aside to reflect on the value of life and the inherent dignity of each person. On Earth, there are many direct threats to vulnerable people. These threats to life cannot be ignored; we are called to defend and protect our most vulnerable. We can stand for life by supporting agencies that offer alternatives and cures to these issues, by expressing our desire to mitigate life in order to provide comfort to everybody who are dying and by educating ourselves on the life issues. Our faith is a call to action and love in the name of **God!!** As members of the faithful, enlightened by **Jesus Christ**, let us speak the truth about life and in doing, bring the light on these issues to the world. **God** created the world in which we live and **Gods** love extends to all people. **God** needs every person to search their heart and soul and find out how they can stand for life. The world needs to hear that every person is valuable because they are harmonized as a result of **The Creator!!!!**

**Book**
*Just Thoughts and Ideas*

**Chapter**
*Reality Check*

*(Never stop using your brain!!)*

I'm so smart I'm a retard!!!!
I'm so good looking I'm ugly!!
I'm so horny I'm a dead fuck!!!!
I'm so pissed I'm happy!!
I'm so broke I'm rich!!!!
I'm so religious I'm supernatural!!
I'm so speechless I'm noisy!!!!
I'm so dead I'm alive!!

**Book**
*Rank Chapter (Larry Page, Serger Brin, web page)*

**Chapter**
*Page Rank*

- Just fucking around with my mind!! Hehehe
- What's after/before a page?

A-Brain ~ 38.4%
B-Eyes ~ 3.9%
C-Heart ~ 3.9%
D-Lungs ~ 3.3%
E-Scrotum ~ 8.1%
F-Bone Marrow ~ 34.3%

Blood ~ 1.6%
Soul ~ 0.1%
Veins ~ 1.6%
Skeleton ~ 1.6%
Muscle ~ 1.6%
Clitoris ~ 1.6%

**Book**
*Money*

**Chapter**
*Exchange*

*Thursday September 26/2013AM*

I was watching Mr. Deeds last night and EDTV the other night, for the first times, but anyways, Mr. Deeds has been playing all night on the menu screen and bills fall down the screen hundreds and hundreds, continuously falling. What if the pile was there for the spending. If we do it the right way it could be out there!!!! **Heaven = Freedom** we either have it in us or we don't. It's a feeling that travels with you your whole life. We want to be free!!

Thinking it over, if you're a believer!! Send this to whomever the fuck you want, if you want to be free, if you want change, if you have the power, if you have the magic, if you love **The Creator....** Send this literature, send, send, send!! I've sent it (September 2013 and December 2014) to Q107, The Toronto Star, The Toronto Sun, CBC, CBS, MGM, LA Times, **Prime Minister Steven Harper,** The Liberal Party, NDP Party, My Lawyer, My File, My Angel etc.... Together we can make a difference!!

**RECEIVE A FREE PASS INTO HEAVEN IF YOU CAN GET TWO PEOPLE TO READ THIS LITERATURE!!!! NEVER FORGET THEIR FIRST AND LAST NAMES!!**

If you don't, receive a *Green Card!!!!*

*Changes are being made, set us free!!*

**Book**
*Learning To Use Special Powers*

**Chapter**
*Seed inside*

So in my literature it says there's an easy way to get into **Heaven.** A male and female temple have a child and that child has to have a child. Bingo your on your way to **Heaven!!** The **Heavens** are watching, that's the first step, remember their names, look into their eyes feel their soul learn their soul. Become known beings!!

**Book**
*Electricity*

*To Be Continued....*

**Chapter**
*Marette*

*To Be Continued...*

**Book**
*Mutation*

**Chapter**
*About-face*

*September 11/2013 7:02pm*

What if we could go from man to woman or woman to man. Look at me I'm male I should have no estrogen, I have low testosterone. I have small balls really small and one is bigger than the other and I can't have kids, I have low sperm count; so this means I have really low testosterone levels. So I should be gay and I am I choose to be with a woman. I'm more like a woman x 10 for eating acid. Human Woman are the sexiest species out there, we have everything on earth in this universe. Dimensions are next!!!!

If you have *Schizophrenia* and have eaten LSD = *Schizomania* = need to escape reality everyday = twice a day!!!! You get Medical Marijuana. **Canada** tested LSD and Cocaine on Mental Heath Patients. That's what I heard and/or seen on television. Or like, it was medication or something.

# LEAF 1 & NOTES

**Book**
*Commitment*

**Chapter**
*My Universes With Dimensions*

1) I promise to work hard my whole life providing for our family
2) I promise to love you and only you
3) I promise to fight for us and I won't let anything stand in our way
4) I promise to give your wants and needs whatever they need and want
5) I promise to give you the time of your life

**Book**
*Uncharged*

**Chapter**
*Evidence/September 9/2013*

*Charges*

Espionage/Espial/Voyeurism/Dreaming - (July 2008)

- Hiding under a blanket and watching a 10 year old temple change into her bathing suit!!

- Foot moved and hit a box before anything happened!!!

- Caught adjusting pants

*Little Girl See Card List!!!!*

*Manifestation*

- What if the temple could get younger? How far would you go back? Could we stop it?

- Spy on the spier had to go undercover to feel the feeler

- Sexual gratification was there, it was not at the top of the list

- The desire of getting caught

- The desire of getting away with it.

- Bin there when I was a kid playing hide and seek

- I was wearing a belt and it was pinching my skin in the prone position adjusted after I got caught. Was not hard a memory is priceless and how you get it is irreplaceable.

**Verdict**

*Fuck you* **Canada** *for keeping it a secret, Thank You!! I Take 100% responsibility!!!*

*See* **Book** *Disgrace,* **Chapter** *666*

**Book**
*Holy Shit*

**Chapter**
*Alzheimer's*

What if you were driving on the highway and your memory and sight was wiped out and you had nothing but the inner soul to use. Could you make it to safety? Hell could be like that all you have are your inner senses with-out presence. Alzheimer's having your memory erased on earth then your presence at the gates of **Hell....** Fuck I don't know. If I could give you a memory chip, I would, but the best I can do is a **Pink Card,** go buy one!!!!

**Book**
*Adam and Eve*

**Chapter**
*Sentence*

What the fuck did they do, to be the ones to start it all, what a premature mind way back then. They never stood a chance at coming to a reasonable reason or did they!!! Wow the punishment of nothing in Heaven or Hell wow what did they do????? They made it to heaven tho maybe!! To be the first humans, makes you think about the other side's eh!!!!!

**Book**
*Others*

**Chapter**
*Teach*

*August 22/2013 10:46pm*

Teach/Educate the over/premature populated planets whatever species we might encounter, we might have to kill!!! We got lucky we might be able to control our problem and save these Universes and bring Dimensions together. One planet at a time. We need earth to last forever like the temple, we control the animal population. life is a walking hormone that can't stop producing life. The human mind is soooo advanced, we have to calm down now or we will be to over populate that we won't know what to do, but kill and kill and kill to share this world our poor grand children. We need to travel and mark our territory. Picture the year 7000 or 106975 or 4099865 or 2050..... Wooow the visions going through my mind I had to pause and fall in love with my mind for five minutes.... Oh **Celestial** I love you soooo much!! Let's just say if **Celestial** and I didn't come together.... This outcome could have been a millennium away and probably a different one, our population is ahead by century plus, I think? 1000-2000 was the millennium of knowledge. We have to train machines don't let them go too far; if they do bring them back without them life has no meaning!!!! Everything is a pet to the human mind, think about it!! We take care of everything on earth!!! Now the universe, then dimensions!!! We Have An Outstanding Angel!!!!

**Book**
*Big Hard Son (Indio)*

**Chapter**
*Read*

If something happens to me, Big Yellow Taxi (Joni Mitchell) I need someone to get my son **Michael** a copy/copies of my literature.... Please, please, please you will get a 500 Gold Cards!! if you are the one and my son reads this!!!! If my son hasn't read it!!!

**Book**
*Disposal*

**Chapter**
*Hungry*

Dump the garbage in the volcano's!!! At some point in the future the make-up of oil might be different because of the garbage in the soil!!! What if we use Hawaii!!!! (the exhaust pipe of Earth)

**Book**
*Spaceship*

**Chapter**
*lasers, bombs, ships*

We need a defense operation!!!!! Not everything is kind; there are two sides to a lot of things!!

There has to be a certain point where we are using just as much oil as the earth is producing. We need Carbon Monoxide (CO) in the air to make the earth move; we can't see blue at night!!! Could you imagine if earth was the only planet that could move 360 degrees?

**Book**
*C4-H12*

**Chapter**
*Gas*

*Gas August 20/Wednesday/2013, $132.9 (GTA) (greater Toronto area)*

Gasoline doesn't go over a $1.40 *Canadian Liter*, spend one (1) day in **Hell** for everyday you have the price over $1.50 *Canadian Liter*. Gasoline doesn't go under $1.20 *Canadian Liter*, spend one (1) day in **Heaven** for everyday you have the price under $1.10 *Canadian Liter*.

*Gas December 13/Saturday/2014, $101.9 (GTA) (greater Toronto area)*
*Gas January 1/Thursday/2015, $94.9 (GTA) (greater Toronto area)*
*Gas January 27/Wednesday/2016, $92.9(GTA) (greater Toronto area)*

**IF WE RUN OUT, WE RUN OUT AND IT WILL BE REPLACED!!! FASTER BECAUSE THEIRS GARBAGE IN THE SOIL**

**Book**
*This Is Some Of My First Writings*

**Chapter**
*Un-Dated Around Five Years*

*(my file at the North Halton Mental Health Clinic has the date)*

CORRUPT LOVE
WE TAKE RESPONSIBILITY FOR OUR LIFE
THERE'S A REASON FOR EVERYTHING
THIS IS OUR HEART
IT CAN/CANNOT BE TO LATE TO CONFESS
FINAL COUNTDOWN

Even people on television/radiation can/cannot be studied. Anybody cannot/will/can be replaced but will they rest in peace/R.I.P.. We can/cannot believe why she's/him or he's/her. We hope you had the time/stay of your life. How well do we know our partner... Why is our/ mine time more valuable than mine/our. What's one thing life can/ cannot live without/with. What is beautiful,,, normal and and and creepy. Why can/will/cannot life win/lose all the time. Why do some temples get cancer/negative. Life can/cannot be sin/sinless. Why is most of the public a honest/fraudulent imitation/phony/realistic. A different half,,, without their gentleman,,, is just an empty space. A lady,,, without their different half,,, is just an empty space. If life can/ cannot see/hear it has a soul. Let someone else go to Montreal then they cannot/will/can teach us what they think/know they learned there. We might go down/up we might go up/down. In thus study please do not/do travel without us.

We are our sponsor/soul mate. How can/cannot humans confess their secret creation to someone else without their wife/husband knowing 1st. We can/cannot give our world to anyone else. IT'S GONE!!!... We give it to us. We gave us tainted romance. We gave us honesty. We gave us space in the summers/winters. We gave us our soul. We gave us our blood. We gave us safety/shelter and we let our mothers/fathers go happy/unhappy. Wee share laughter/crying and heartache/joyfulness together so far/near. We made each other we know what's correct/false. Now we are giving yourself/us our life line. Our life line has our optimum schedule, voice our/yours opinion to our life line listen/observe. Start from where ever we/u want, have complete/hunger. Be us/yourself.

Every life that has touched our path. Has made us into the holy grail we will continue/backwards to be. We feel alive/scared that our world wont ignore/accept its liaison. Our #1/number 3 love is us and NAME. Unaware/knowing what the future/past can/cannot give us whatever kind of manipulation/love we want if we put our mind/ body to work/rest. But we want to feel 2 worlds become one/three

Life isn't too short we have eternity to spend together. We want to see us every time before we sleep and see each other's smile when we wake. Let's move forward jointly we are the best weave eternally. We are trying so hard to endeavor each other. We are found/lost and incomplete/complete. We want to keep calling us baby and buzzing our number. It takes speed/arrest to change 0.000000 and so on, 1. No one cannot/will/can explain how small/long this number is. It takes time -3-2-10123 and so forth,,, to understand why our sponsor/ soul mates life is turning out the way it is. No one can/cannot explain how large/reverse this # could be. Whatever way we want to look/ find at this that's not the apex. This can/cannot be translated

--- We/different are best friends we want to experience it all together.
--- Our mothers/fathers are under supervised/general/labor visitation/employment.
--- We/different are going to get our child and spend the night/day with him/her we will drop her/him off at school/unschooled.
--- We/different can/will/cannot promise us anything/something. We will try our best to spend eternity without/with each other.
--- We/different are tired we need to go away and make a bloodline><family tree = 3,,,6,,,9,,,ect./odd/even/odd/even etc.
--- We/different are not crazy, sick or mentally whatever we/you want to call it.
--- This is our world, no one is going to take it from us again.
--- WE USED love trying to find a fairytale. Now we think we are capable of give our princes/prince a fairytale ending.
--- Baby we need our loving we are each others sunshine/moonlight
--- One +\-1= English/French or words/blindness or independence/ with or solo/wings. Im going on with our life with/without us. We are fucking free/two/0. gods dam you.
--- We/different are not perfect there's no I or i in team.
--- subject to change... WE ARE CANADIAN!!!... Happily ever after together...

SHERBERY TIME-
TAKE CARE OF YOUR TEMPLE-
50/50 WIFE/HUSBAND

The first little person created by a man and woman get their souls to make them husband and wife. The first/third/fifth etc. Child doesn't have to choose a soul they are born with two the the mothers and father.

What if you could choose to commit suicide/die of natural causes. It could be out there if you want it. You have to do it the right way and raise your child/children the right way.

Does half the universe rotate around the sun at the same distance or does the universe rotate into the sun. If the sun went out what would you do??? How does it get its fuel is it from other planets. Do you really want your grand children to be born in the year 1000000?? Numbers can go straight to the sun or reverse to the black hole or we can make or go around the sun. Do not make it leap and try to stop time by making it equal.

NEWTONS FIRST LAW

A body continues to maintain its state of rest or uniform unless acted upon by a external unbalanced force = TODAY'S TIMELINE
INERTIA = Resistance to change reluctance to move or act, hesitant or unwilling SHERBERY TIMELINE

NEWTONS SECOND LAW

The force on an object is equal to the mass of the object multiplied by its acceleration = north and south poles (no I in team) east and west (no I in team)

NEWTONS THIRD LAW

To every action there is an equal and opposite reaction = Light coming from the sun, elements going to the sun (fuel). From a certain point in time the closer planets get to the sun the more elements are sucked by the sun. We will never find out if life exited on Mars the elements are gone, it is too close to the sun. There has to be a certain point in time where everything will continue to go around the earth or missing it avoiding it. Or we can continue to have the earth rotate on its core moving closer to the sun until we are extinct. If there is no more food there is one way to survive.

We had to come this far to this point in time. Computers work off numbers. The human brain works off letters, numbers and symbols. Computers can be defeated.

BY: DND CALWOOD

My Psychiatrist asked me what I want and I *said "A Credit Card With No Limit."* (Nickelback)

**Book**
*Q107*

**Chapter**
*Worth*

$999,999,999,999.99 Canadian Cash divided by 2000 years (nothing is worth more than **My Celestial**) hold on to a 1977 *Canadian Penny*. Bring it with you if you have $999,999,999,999.99. Starts Sunday August 18,2013 12:00pm. Or my signature is worth a *Canadian Penny* and it's free. If you can get the cheque before this book is finished? You will get a **Platinum Card** and your blood family will be taken care of forever!!!! Generation After Generation!! One owner only!!

**Book**
*Quest*

**Chapter**
*I feel safe*

IT CAN/CANNOT HAPPEN TO ANYONE
HOW I VIEW AND LISTEN TO MY WORLD
PREMEDITATED/PERFECTIONIST

This is my paper trail....
There's lettering/numbering/symboling throughout....
It's my turn to say no....
There are the things I've been trying to figure out with my mysterious life....

Religion is a way of life....

I had to find my beliefs and way before I become one....

It's not unusual to see and hear me cry....

I cried writing these....

I cried reading them....

I might cry reading them once more, I might not, that's not the point....

I don't know if I can make eye contact, that's not the point....

I can look at myself in the mirror and say "wow," that's not the point....

If you try to manipulate my better half I will make your life living hell....

It's over, it's all over....

I will not lie down and die, I will survive....

These souls can/cannot change,,,,,.....

May the magnetism be with us....

I can/cannot make this stuff up....

Either way I found my world....

Backspace.... Download manipulated/self-governed restricted/unrestricted trail,,, Spacebar....

In the end was it worth it....

Life gets more exciting with each passing day....

**Book**
*Get The Papers Started*

**Chapter**
*Wendy*

If **Celestial** dies before me, I want to be put down by injection, there's evidence in my literature that proves there might be an *Unknown* and I don't want my wife to go alone!! I need help!!!! I will go to court for this, the longer this takes the longer we are apart!! We need to dream our cremation!!!!

**Book**
*Will*

**Chapter**
*Death*

If **Celestial** and I break up, I will not harm myself. I always manage to pray Sunday most of the times at a *Catholic Church* somewhere. If we are together and something happens to **Our Angel.** I will seriously consider killing myself. I will not let **My Wife** die alone, if **My Pumpkin** passes away before me!!!

All I ask is if I die before **Celestial** preserve my body until **Celestial** dies if **Our Angel** dies, then cremate us together!!!!!!!! **My Son** continuing my work through-out this process!!

It's totally her decision just cremate me with the opposite sex!!!!! Then the **Platinum Card** is carried on, choose a good one **Honey!! Please stay with me forever until you're ready to take me to Heaven with you, my sperm needs to be the last to ever enter you!! "Condoms" you say, I say, "I wouldn't have sex if I were you", I'll buy you a dildo, there are ways around everything.**

**Book**
*Recycling*

**Chapter**
*The Human Body*

1- *Re-Use Body Parts* - valuable ones, we need most of our temple and eyes (Two **Gold Cards,** one for each eye)(inheritance after your temple is cremated) . You will be compensated whatever we can use. Cremating the remaining
2- See **Book** *-25 Chapter Three Public.* This is what happens if you don't get married!!! We use your parts.... If we use them!!
   A) Here's a picture of all the woman that died today. **Celestial** if this is your wish, that are not married. Pick the prettiest one with your eyes. Everybody has standards, I'm not a bad looking man, just cremate me with a woman with the same prettiness!!!!

**B)** Choose my clothes and hair style and perfume or the other cologne.

**C)** My eyes open, standing, sitting, lying down eyes closed, change and clean me once a week if I'm preserved. I want people, **Our Angel** to come and see me. With glass in-between us I don't care!!!! Take care of **Celestial** and **I** please!!

**D)** Q107 playing on the P.A.

## Book
*Look Out*

## Chapter
*Auditors*

- Are everywhere $200,000 *Canadian Cash* a year, One Gold Cards on Spot (all expenses paid for, then give it back, if you retire or the card runs out)!!
- Minimum Wage $15.00 *Canadian Cash* an hour
- Skill Trade $30 *Canadian Cash* an hour with papers e.g. Welder, Tool &Die, Millwright, Mechanic, Paralegal, Accountants, Managers etc.
- Doctors $100 *Canadian Cash* an hour
- Lawyers $50 *Canadian Cash* an hour

Royalties are the way to go; I once had someone tell me my book would be good for Psychology classes in Universities. (Psychiatrist $200 *Canadian Cash* an hour) So I Said to My Friend "you're telling me my book will be studied and purchased for generations after generations" He said "YES" I said "sweet"

- See **Gold Card**
- See **Platinum Card**
- See **Silver Card**
- See **Bronze Card**
- See **Pink Card**
- Body Guards can only use cards when they are with me or **Celestial** and our **Three Sons**, when outside *North America* or the *Philippines!!* $500,000 *Canadian Cash* a year *Canadian Cash*, once the balance runs out on the **Gold Card** or you run out, you will be replaced!!!

**Book**
*Whatever Really*

**Chapter**
*Cannibalism*

Wow yippy I can go out and get a child bring them home, have my way with them, fry them up and eat them. Before **Hell** is gone, its 2013, add a million, so let's say I eat someone June 18/973261 so I only have to serve 28751 years minus a second and then be free. Yes and serve my life alone in a cell on Earth with nothing.... No pen, No paper nothing!!!! Omg **hell** no after that I would want to be the one to re-write **Hell**!!!!!!!!!! Nope no thanks!! There's ways around everything "say what" boogers, ear wax, toe nails, peach fuzz, skin is food times two if you're married mix and match for different taste. (See **Book** *Food & Water to eat if there's no food....*)

- *Eat one pound of your scabs and get a **Silver Card**, you have 10 years to collect them!!*

**Book**
*Disgrace*

**Chapter**
*666*

- **Olive Omnipotent** (1 **Hell** day) 1 day = from the time *I* die to the time *Celestial* dies and I want her to live a healthy life on earth being faithful to me with our memories, if we die. There's no *Purgatory* for me (so my soul can't make love to **Celestial,** until our souls collide and she brings me to *Heaven!!* it's a naughty vision I would have had for the rest of my life!!! Stand beside **Satan,** *The Creator* or *Celestial*? (I will rip you both apart to get to *My Celestial Being*)(*With Medical Marijuana on Earth*) (I'm a *coward,* I want to sacrifice *My Angel* first, and then it's off to la la land for me with a car, a parking spot, a case of beer, a bag of weed, Baconator with lettuce, tomato, onion with extra Baconator sauce on the side with a poutine and chili cheese nachos, chili and cheese on the side and a large coke with a hose with and a full tank of gas!!)(so in reality today people think One **Hell** Day is longer than an *Earth* day, so if **Celestial** dies before me, I could make One **Hell** Day, Less than an *Earth* Day, the sky could fucking change color man!!)

- If you can serve 25 years 13 hours 15 minutes and 06 seconds or have and still alive in a *North American* or *European* Jail receive a **Gold Card**
- If you can go to **Hell** for seven days or more and come back to earth in the same temple receive a **Platinum Card**

## Book
*The Temples Eye And Mind*

## Chapter
*Curiosity x Infinity*

I was reading "My last name was **Opportune,** during World War II my Grandfather changed our last name to **Omnipotent,** because there's Jewish blood running though our family. So umm.... I've had a sperm analyst done. I'm seven and the normal guy is 21." I totally slowed down my reading and focused on the letters and movement, knowing what I was reading and thinking and missing **My Angel** at the same time "that **Pink Cards** = 5 **Silver Cards**". Then I realized what I was doing and lost concentration!! It happens with everything, just not with this book!!!!!!!!!! **Celestial** is always on mind with me 24/7!! *Team work!!!!*

## Book
*Neighbor*

## Chapter
*Elevator*

We should go to Mars and have a cumfest (Come Together)(The Beatles)!!! Adam and Eve had to start somewhere.... Earth was planed (oxygen had to be here) we have the technology to build an atmosphere!! The imaginary line, what is it? Every planet has one!!

## Book
*One Giant Leap For Mankind (Neil Armstrong)*

## Chapter
*Heaven*

Must read this on your 16th birthday at midnight starts the first day of the month after your birthday, your life will continue after the last day of the month before your birthday!!!! Go get your dreams!! I love you!!!!!! You have $250,000 *Canadian Cash* a gift from **The Higher Power!!!!!!!!** **CARDS START AT AGE 30!!** It's yours no one can tell you how to spend it but there are rules!!! Thank you for being born!!

1) Must give $1000 *Canadian Cash* to charity your choice
2) Must work or perform community service (25 hours a month) until age 25
3) Must keep at least $100 *Canadian Cash* in the Power Account (cannot make deposits) until age 25 then withdraw the balance and close the account and give it to charity (the balance)
4) If you don't follow the rules you have to pay it back after you turn 30, you have 20 years to have a balance of $100,000 *Canadian Cash* in the Power Account then give it to charity or spend one year in a NCR facility before age 80!!! Then you get your card if your name is on one of the lists so the faster you get $100,000 or do your time. The earlier you get your card!!

## Book
*Time Travel*

## Chapter
*2600 BC*

Stonehenge where do we start or is this where we/they come back? We need to chip the human body. I don't go anywhere with-out a body guard (body guards travel ALONE!!!)

**Book**
*32*2'N 31*13'E*

**Chapter**
*Pyramids*

What if the pyramids are a gateway (teleport) to other universes (galaxy's) ?¿

**Book**
*0123456789*

**Chapter**
*XI, Satellites*

The satellites are watching me, so be good when you're around me. They want to be the first to know!! I have no choice our angel holds a **Platinum Card***!!!!* I'm good!! Together forever.... We will find away!! Smile **Honey** you're a dream come true!!

**Book**
*Unit*

**Chapter**
*Total*

-forever changing, we need answers.

**Book**
*?*

**Chapter**
*13, Freedom*

The Meaning Of Life, What a dirty trick, What did we do¿?....let's find out? We've been abused by the *criminal system, family law system and the mental health system!* United we stand, divided we fall!!

Hanging *Jesus?* he's tired lay him down let him rest!!! Free *Jesus!!* Then put him back up.. Clean *Jesus!!* Hug, kiss, hold *Jesus* close to the heart!! We love you *Jesus!!*

We Are Ahead By A Century (The Tragically Hip) lets freeze time and make our future!! Everything we do we do for love!!

**Book**
*Floating*

**Chapter**
*The Human Body*

**(The Boy Who Could Fly)**

*To be continued....*

**Book**
*3012, Motion*

**Chapter**
*121, Earth*

This will be the last copy for awhile, need to collect my thoughts and view more things. So they make sense... Things are getting straight I trust you all.... Together Forever!!

Could you imagine if we could move the Earth by the littlest 0.000000000000000000000000000000001 or the greatest 131127442456788854335577666.0 around everything!! As a team!! We are losing our ozone layer!! (I understand its the $CO_2O$ or whatever in the air that's killing the ozone)

**Book**
*A True Love Story*

**Chapter**
*777,* **Olive & Celestial**

This is real, something extraordinary is possible. That might do us some good. Are you ready for a miracle??
Let's free *Purgatory,* the harmony of existence..

The secret plan was cleverly contrived. These works are the efflorescence of her/his genius!!

Changes everywhere....
You might think your reading the same thing over but you're not!! I will send copies when I feel comfortable.
For instance "I can die in peace" was changed too "We can rest in peace" and "Female goddess (together forever) male = child (life) was changed to "Female **Goddess** *(together forever)* Male **God** = *(child* **life***)*

My heart is back. **Honey Celestial (My Angel)..** Is still in my life. Good and bad we manage to get through it!! Together Forever.
My last name was **Opportune;** during World War II my Grandfather changed our last name to **Omnipotent,** because there's Jewish blood running though our family. So umm.... I've had a sperm analyst done. I'm seven and the normal guy is 21. I had the test done four or five years ago. Lungs checked. There's a lot that has to be taken care of!! Like, **Celestial**, Me, special family and friends, everyone, everything before this gets started!!
**Celestial** and I will represent **Canada** with class. Made In **Canada!!** We will never forget the true meaning of love.. I live in the best country in the world. Canada is #1. Everything I know, I thank **The Creator** and **Canada!!**
I've served over two years in the reserves, over a year in jail, have had about 45 jobs. My service number is **A51 583 223**, my offender ID number is **1112356245**, my S.I.N. is **894 635 651**, My ODSP member I.D. number is **65824652** These numbers will follow

me the rest of my life in **Canada...** My knowledge of the armed forces, criminal system and total work career, I owe to my hands-on education, I've read one book, my whole life. It was "The Thirteenth Floor" I think I was in grade three all I know is I lived in a co-op in Brampton, Ontario, **Canada.** Until grade nine.

My Mom My Lord Hannah let me drop out of high school in grade nine. She was a single mother of two. I can't remember what age but I lived in the co-op my best-friend Tom Stafford growing up. After I finished kicking snow at him from behind and saying some bad things. While we were walking to school. We didn't talk much after that. But if I didn't make my choices that lead me here, we wouldn't be where we are today. Everybody has a best-friend from child hood, Tom would have been mine, we did everything together. I remember drinking my mom's Peach Schnapps and Vodka. We were at my place having a sleep over. I don't know where my mom was, probably with John and Lisa (Toms Parents) or on a date. I knew where she was, I just can't remember. Or doing whatever our parents did, we trusted our parents. I don't remember much about the night. I was showing Tom that I heard we can water down my mom's alcohol and smoke her cigarette butts. Tom didn't drink or smoke, I don't think but he took care of me. I pissed all over the kitchen. I'm pretty sure Tom cleaned it up. We didn't talk much about it after that. We were a great team.

What we did together I did with my son **Michael.** He's my Jesus! I took my sons pacifier and bottle away, I toilet trained my son. I taught my son how to ride a bike, I do school projects with my son, I build forts in the woods, igloos in the winter, go on hikes, climb trees and play sports, with my son and his friends. There's a lot I can teach my son, there's a lot he will not get away with too.

Then we moved to Georgetown, Ontario with Chris. Chris is one of the smartest men I know, I've looked up to him my whole life. I remember his car rolling down the hill on the circle at Mondragon Circle in Brampton. He was running after it. He got it just before it crashed into a townhouse but it took down a fence first. I always thought to myself "how do I get as smart as him". We moved without my sister Sarah. My sister was kicked out when she was 14.

I worked two part-time jobs while going to high school in Georgetown, grades weren't the greatest but I passed. I supported my habits. Going to School, Working, Driving, Sex, Smoking, Drinking doing Drugs, Partying, Smoking Weed, had it 95% of the time, (never sold drugs, just hooked my friends up for a high) going to school high everyday meeting my high school girlfriend at school for more highs. There was this church right beside G.D.H.S (Georgetown District High School), the church opened there door for the teenagers, it was open from periods two to four, most of the time later!! There was a pool table, card tables, TV, VHS player, ping-pong table, fridge, canteen. Getting high drinking skipping class, going to Open Door. Getting sex almost every day, most of the time more than once, I remember having a party, lines in the dining room, knifes in the kitchen, beer, alcohol, weed everywhere, Pink Floyd The Wall on TV in the living room, acid eyes everywhere. My high school girlfriend and I and two other couples went in my room, closed the door turned off the lights and we started to have an intimate moment with the person we were with (NO ONE said *switch*) the smell, the feelings, the sounds, the visions, the imagination running though our minds, the connection between all of us was out of this world. Having sex six times in one night on acid, booze, weed. Was a work out.

I moved to Georgetown in September grade nine so I should have been in grade eleven, because I failed grade three and dropped out for a year. I started working full-time after I dropped out in grade nine, worked full time packing those white snakes for dyers in the laundry room, in boxes. Got fired for cutting the wire on the automatic tape machine. (I was bored) I cried when I got fired. Went to the washroom for a couple of minutes. Then I walked out, went to the bus stop, then went home. It was my first full-time job.

Then I got this job as a shoe shiner at a golf club in Brampton (good tips). I remember at the golf club, we closed all the doors and windows. In the shoe shine room.

This other guy dropped out of high school the same time I did and we got the job together job hunting. (though school because our moms signed us out of high school because we were under age at 14 or 15) Anyways Paul and I cut all the tips of sulfur off hundreds of matches and put them in a jar, lit one match and threw it in the jar and put the lid back on quickly. The jar started spinning around and the lid blew off and smoke went everywhere and this blue flame came shooting out of the jar (what a kool dragon). We looked at each other and said "what are we going to do?". We kept the room closed up, tried everything to get rid of the smell and smoke, before someone notices and someone did.

The fire department was called, the smoke disappeared before the fire truck came and the smell wasn't that bad. We acted like we knew nothing about it and got away with it!!

My Mom My Lord Hannah moved to Georgetown a month before me, before school started, so I quit the golf club and took a month off and lived in the co-op by myself before the move in September. My Lord Hannah was going from one place to the other, but slept in Georgetown. I know this because I beat Super Mario 3 in a month.

Georgetown was where I was introduced to drugs and alcohol. LSD was my drug of choice in high school, I remember eating it almost every week-end, writing my grade 12 english exam on it, peeking out! (Pink Floyd-The Wall was amazing)(Woodstock also).

My Father Numen Omnipotent and My Lord Hannah got married 1969, they also went to Woodstock, don't eat the brown acid!!!

My high school girlfriend and I broke up, with four credits remaining in grade 12, so I dropped-out.

I lost my license when I was twenty-one for impaired driving. Drinking all day with three buddies and we decided to go to Hooters in Brampton. On our way home, I blacked-out, hopped a curb landed in some guys driveway push their cars forward and took down part of their garage. My buddy said "run" but I tried to get away. Didn't get to far. The cops pulled me over 50ft ahead and charged me with (DUI, driving with no insurance and failure to remain) and put me in the drunk tank for the night. My Camaro Berlinetta was a right off!! My buddies hopped a cab back to Georgetown and got caught. They talked to the police at the scene lol!! That's what I heard?

Chris picked me up the next morning and asked me to take him to the scene he said "I wouldn't want to wake up to that".

Then I went back to high school when I was 23 and took a military co-op for four credits, joined the reserves after the co-op (lived off my severance pay from Magna), my Grandfather has pictures with Frank Stronach with $1,000,000 horses

Then My Son **Michael** was conceived in Burlington Ontario, in a hotel room. Born May 2/2000. I had the week-end off in august 1999. I was doing my basic training in Meaford, Ontario. We had the week-end off, before the final test. A 15km rucksack, full gear physical training exercise. 15km of discipline, the last 100m a fireman carry over the shoulders, one km each. Grabbing whoever we could get, soldiers were everywhere in front, behind, beside all over. I found a man my size and we made it to the end!!!!

During the summer training, I was a section leader for my room. There was about 10 of us in a section. A soldier was opening his jackknife and stabbed me in the leg, down I went grabbing my leg. Private Shapiro said "oh fuck did I zap you" it felt like an electric shock going through my leg. It took two hours to stitch up. The military was in training for the summer!!!!

After my son was conceived Rachelle and I decided, I should stayed in the reserves and work full-time. Because the training was out east or west for what I wanted to do and we didn't want to relocate. I wanted to use my hands fixing things (full-time)

Being in and out of jail for two years, my longest bid was 8 months. I was in jail for; my record is:

Record (this is what I was charged with, this is what the public can find out, there are ways around everything, if you really want to know my bad side, you can find out?)

**A)** Theft Under $1000
- 1994
Sentence
~1 year probation

**A)** DUI
- 1995
**B)** Driving With-out Insurance
- 1995
**C)** Failure To Remain
- 1995
Sentence
~1 year license suspension
~$500 fine
~$500 fine

**A)** Criminal Harassment
- October 2008
**B)** Mischief Under $5000
- October 2008
**C)** Breach Of Bail
- February 2009
Sentence
~74 days in jail
~40 days in the hospital
~2 year probation
~Banned from Milton

**A)** Breach Of Probation x2
- September 2009
**B)** Breach Of Probation x6
- November 2009
Sentence
~70 days in jail
~110 days in the hospital
~3 year probation

**A)** Breach Of Probation x4
- June 2010
**B)** Death Threats
- September 2010
Sentence
~8 months in jail

**A)** Impaired Driving (drug)
July 2011
**B)** Breach Of Probation x3
July 2011
Sentence
~Charges Withdrawn

We are all here for the same reason, to do our time. You go your way, **My Wife** and *I* will go our way, life's a dirty trick!! What the fuck did we do? Years and years of punishment, murder after murder and incest after incest.

*(Come together right now!!! Life's is nothing but a dream)*

Venting on paper in jail (*death threats*) I only kill for food, or if they bug me! It's a dog eat dog world. I was charged with Criminal Harassment for; a bunch of text messages, e-mails and voice mails. I have never laid my hands on a woman in a violent way, the messages were about, how could a beautiful family, two people that loved each other so much, that brought life into this world. How could it go so wrong? (85% my fault) I did a lot of bad things to My Sons Mother, if you really want to know, just ask Rachelle, she knows everything!! I Told My Sons Mother..

*In jail;*
I was with murders, men that killed their mothers, men that kill their girlfriends, men that killed their daughters, teenager killing their grandfather because he molested children, rapists, some man tied a 10 year old up to a tree and had anal sex with him, robbers, a man tried to use tranquilizer darts on guards that drive the armored trucks that carry money..... All on my range. I knew nothing about the criminal system back then. The guards asked "do you need protective custody?" I said "yes"! Once you go PC you can't go GP, (I didn't know) if someone passes you, while walking around, working whatever. If someone from GP notices your face around the jail and you're in PC you can't go from Protective Custody to General Population, you could lose your life or get seriously hurt. Inmates should be allowed one cigarettes at yard if you have them smoke them (no smoking inside)(two weeks no yard!) Save and smoke use it as a bid in a game of cards. Have fun!!!

Oh and the hole been there!!! I smoked tobacco and weed in jail, mind you there was a lock down and search done but I got high and had a good night sleep. Until the morning. I lost my job as a server in jail after that, a half ounce of weed was found on another range. A Green judge is a "Worship" and a red judge is a "Your Honour"

When I was released from jail, I had the shirt on my back and the pants I was wearing with jail shoes. Having the engagement ring in my pocket. I made my way back to Milton, form a shelter in Brampton. I remember sleeping at Rogers Center, covered with brown leaves, for warmth! Pan-handling the next morning at Union

Station for my bus ride back to the shelter. I got $300 for the black diamonds in Burlington at a pawn shop. Put it down for a down payment on a car (my money maker). I was charged with impaired driving (drug) again!! (Summer of 2011). I was living in Milton with Joe renting a room from him. I was partying at my sisters, I was drinking but not much, I was snorting Clozapine and Wellbutrin. (Just kidding we need humor when writing a book) Went down to my car for a five hour sleep, woke-up and made my way home. I was pulled over at the first set of lights by the police (3am). The cop shined the flashlight at my face and asked "what is that orange powder around your nose?" I said "it must be Doritos I had some chips before I went to bed I must have rubbed my nose and the residue from the chips must have came off my finger and stuck to my nose". the ambulance was called and they released me!! They still charged me with breaches and the impaired charged. My lawyer got me off. I've been having nothing but problems with cars because of the black diamonds. I had a house, two cars, a pool, wife and son and family pets. I was making close to $70,000 a year working from 3am to 4:30pm Monday to Friday, Saturdays 3am to 10am, Sunday 4am to 9am. For four years. I supported my habits, on my paper route I remember putting beer in snow banks to get them cold, 26er of vodka under my seat, drinking them while I was inserting and putting a rubber band around The Faraway Post, Q107 always on the radio!! so I could throw them from the sidewalk (some papers landed on the roof, always had pot with me!!!!)

Then **Celestial, My Princess**. It was love at first sight for me. As soon as I made eye contact, I knew **Celestial** was the one and I knew if she gave me chance. I would not let her down. We met April 26/2013. I've never had 100% of a woman; I feel I'm almost there with **Celestial.** I treat My Angel like a Lady. She has every right to have to have a fairytale ending. This is real!!

**My Princess**

What else could I say about a *"Stunning Phoenix"*....

She wants true love, doesn't need a father....

She sits there full of life and love, she's still alive....

Is she satisfied, everywhere she looks, she sees wanting eyes....

She needs a magnetic connection, men are trying to reach her, but there's no easy way to find true love....

She doesn't need any more education, with her strikingly attractive mind....

*This world is hers for the taking!!!!*
**(Queen Celestial)**

*(Look at the royal family what a escapade!!*
*They forgot their roots look what got them there) makes you think eh!!*

I always wanted something but never knew that all I ever wanted was more and more of **Celestial!!** I just want to stay by her day and night. Her cute smile and her happy laughter attracted me to her, but her caring loving heart is the reason why I want to spend the rest of my life with **Celestial.** The best feeling I get is when I see her face early morning and when I dream about her by night.

loving her forever and ever is a dream come true (eternity you and I!!) Her love has changed me so very much. People say I am a different person now but I'm still the same. I guess when you fall in love, everything changes. I will be at peace because I have known My Soul mate and have understood the true meaning of love. There is not enough that I can write about **Celestial,** but I want to end this page by saying that with all my heart and soul and mind, I really, truly, do Love **My Honey!!**

(I Love You **Celestial** XOXO)

I was baptized *Catholic;* I'm not a practicing *Catholic.* I really have no religion, I believe **Jesus Christ** died on the cross. I do take communion when I go to a *Catholic* Church.

After My Father Numen Omnipotent Committed Suicide, I think I was three or four, when My Father Numen Omnipotent broke on through to the other side! (The Doors) the rest of my family moved to Bramalea, from Windsor where I was born.

My whole life I finally found what I've been looking for (U2).... I have my high school diploma, I've been to tech college and chef college. I am a Creationist. We/they are the only true Schizophrenics. I am not violent or malicious. I've been in one fight and Chris's nephew beat me, when I lived in the co-op!!!

*Dedicated to:*
**Honey CAR MELA** My Universes with Dimensions!! And to every thought that has processed on earth (the brain)... Control the animal population, let's eat in peace!! But most of all to the meaning of life::::: Meat should be expensive, it takes a lot to get to **Heaven!!**

*Looking back*

**Book**
*6-9, 666666-999999999*

**Chapter**
*69-69, 2ofus4ever69*

Christianity is one of the world's largest religions, with over 2.5 billion adherents, known as Christians. Christians believe **Jesus** is the Son of **God** and the savior of humanity who's coming as Christ or the Messiah was written in the Old Testament.

Judaism generally views **Jesus** as one of a number of false messiahs who have appeared throughout history. Jews believe they are the chosen ones, through **God!!**

Muslims believe that **God** is one and incomparable and the purpose of existence is to love and serve **God.** Muslims also believe that Islam is the complete and universal version of a primordial faith that was revealed at many times and places before, including through Abraham, Moses and **Jesus**, whom they consider prophets.

Hinduism is often called the "oldest living religion". Hinduism includes a wide spectrum of laws and prescriptions of "daily morality" based on karma, dharma, and societal norms.

Sikhism was not only formed to protect the Hindus, but all living things. A way of life and philosophy well ahead of its time when it was founded over 500 years ago, Sikhism preaches a message of devotion and remembrance of **God** at all times, truthful living, equality of mankind.

The Rastafarian movement is an African-based spiritual ideology that arose in the 1930s in Jamaica. Rastafarians believe Haile Selassie is *God,* and that he will return to Africa and free members of the black community who are living in exile as the result of colonization and the slave trade. Rastafarians accept much of the Bible, although they believe that its message has possibly been corrupted.

To many, Buddhism goes beyond religion and is more of a philosophy or 'way of life'. It is a philosophy because philosophy 'means love of wisdom' and the Buddhist path can be summed up as:

(**1**) to lead a moral life,
(**2**) to be mindful and aware of thoughts and actions, and
(**3**) to develop wisdom and understanding.

*Religion is fascinating!!! We believe everything!!!*

*We are love*
*We are magic*
*We are beauty*
*We are pure*
*We are perfect*
*We are endlessness*
*We are evolving*
*We are mindful*
*We are energy*
*We are vision*
*We are human*
*We are vivid*
*We are walking life*
*We are elusive*
*We are playing*
*We are spirit*
*We are internal*

*We are external*
*We are breathing*
*We are dedicated*
*We are connected*
*We are electric*
*We are radiant*
*We are galactic*
*We are unity*
*We are psychedelic*
*We are infinite*
*We are me*

**Book**
*Team Work*

**Chapter**
*Caught In The Middle*

I can only teach the teachers!!!! It's a long process, it took 40 years to get this far. My better half is the most powerful woman alive; she has control of my brains!! WHOA finally!! (You Had My Heart And Soul) (Adele) I will never go to family court (what a fucking joke), My Sons Mother got all my rights when I was in jail. I didn't stand a chance. I couldn't defend myself (I can go to one court but not the other, it's whatever!!) She can fucking keep them. Fucking coward!! She needs a biff on the forehead! I've seen my son three times in five years!! The first time I went to jail for it! Its whatever!! I just wanted to hug and kiss my son and see his friends and Tito!!!! I need a third party... Lmao!! Okay Canada raise my son with-out me!! What are you going to do put me in jail or the hospital forever... I will find away!! I will adapt!!! *Celestial* is keeping me alive!! Take ***My Angel*** away from me and I will wipe you out of *existence!!* My son is one thing ***My Wife*** is another!!!! You can't control my mind wherever I am! If I have to start over **Hell** will freeze over! If its *Celestial's* decision, I can live with that!! We are in a relationship!!!! All I'm saying is please take care of *Celestial*, we are a team!!!!

**Book**
*Generations*

**Chapter**
*Public*

- If you give life to a pure child, that child gets $500,000 *Canadian Cash*. Brother and Sisters get $250,000 *Canadian Cash*. If the second child is the opposite sex from the first child. He/she also receives $500,000 *Canadian Cash*. On their first child's birthday.
- If you have the name Bill, win an extra $10,000 cash *Canadian Money*..
- If You have the name Shakira, win an extra $25,000 cash *Canadian Money*..
- If you have the name **Melaya** Today (July 7/2013) win $1,000,000.75 cash *Canadian Money*. If you have a girl and name the child **Melaya** after the game starts, that child will receive $20,000.75 *Canadian Money* on their 10th birthday, If you have a boy and name that child **Turbo** after the game starts, that child will receive $20,000.50 *Canadian Money* on their 12th birthday any other names will receive $10,000.25 *Canadian Money* on their 15th birthday..
- If you have HIV receive a **Silver Card**
- if you have AIDS receive a **Gold Card**
- if you have herpes two weeks in jail, you have to serve before you know what?
- Murder (eg. Death Penalty) or Rape (eg. Widowed) - 1/2 eternity in **Hell** (minus one **Hell** day)
- Cocaine-365 days in jail, Saturdays and Sundays in the hole with Q107 playing on the PA (0.1-1kilo = 1 year)
- LSD-6 months in jail no yard Saturday and Sunday (1 sheet = 1000 = 1-1000 = 6 months)(1-1000 pills = 6 months)(1-10ml = 6 months)
- Crack-9 months in jail no yard, Mondays at noon you will put a piece of crack in a condom up your ass the size of a golf ball until Wednesday at midnight, you are constipated for that time you must give it all back or add 5 years!!! (0.1-golf ball size = 9 months)

- Body Parts ~ You will be compensated, the more important the part, the more you get. If you've lost or are missing any body part or more than one!! For any reason...

e.g.
- Blood (Free)
- Flesh o-oz $1000
- Colon $1,500,000
- Testicle $50
- Breast $1,250,000
- Finger $10,000
- Foot $30,000
- Lung $50,000,000
- Hand $25,000
- Vein 0-1" $250
- Liver $20,500,000
- Trachea $1,000,000
- Heart five **Silver Cards**
- You must pay *Canadian Cash* for body parts if you need them, same price!! If you can get them?
- Magic Mushrooms are legal (Friday Nights from 6:00pm to 11:00pm)(Saturdays 24hrs) take a taxi!
- Marijuana is legal (no driving park the car)
- 16 years old ~ Drive
- 19 years old ~ Drink Alcohol
- 18 years old ~ Smoke Marijuana
- 25 years old ~ Smoke Cigarettes
- 30 years old ~ Magic Mushrooms
- Welfare $1000 a/month *Canadian Cash*
- Disability minimum wage 40hr week *Canadian Cash*
- Pension 65 years old minimum wage 40hr week *Canadian Cash*

**Book**
*Summary*

**Chapter**
*More rules of the **Money Cards***

**1**-You must give your money away, if you die or the bank owns everything or whatever assets that's not in your will. Excluding the **Platinum Card** (the country owns everything) if you die or go over your max!!!

**Book**
*Planet*

**Chapter**
*Continents*

- $250,000 cash *Canadian Money* to everyone to start; you can spend it however you want!! See **Book** *One Giant Leap For Mankind (Neil Armstrong)* **Chapter** *Heaven* for your rules if your birthday is before oops after May 2/2016!! Let the games begin. July 31/2013!! Go get your dreams!! Good luck!! Play the game!!
- Canada gets a four or five day weekend!!! Use the floating holiday wisely!!! We can make it happen!!
- **Canada** gets a seven dollar bill $7
- **Philippines** gets free health care, welfare, ODSP, pension, no wait, everybody gets it
- If you have over $100,000,000 (August 10,2013) receive One **Gold Card**
- *Pennies, Nickels and Dimes* are obsolete in Canada
- If you have over $1,000,000,000 receive *Two* **Gold Cards** (August 10,2013)!!
- Under $100,000,000 (August 10,3013) receive a **Silver Card** for every $10,000,000 up to $100,000,000
- Under $10,000,000 (August 10,2013) receive a **Bronze Card** for every $1,000,000 up to $10,000,000
- Under $1,000,000 receive a **Pink Card** for every $1000 up to $1,000,000

*Platinum Cards Go To:*
- **Celestial Bloom**
- **Michael Bloom-Omnipotent**
- **Ryan Bloom-Omnipotent**
- **Richard Bloom-Omnipotent**
- **Paul Diamonds first child**
- **Little Girl (a daughter we might not ever have)**

*Gold Cards Go To:*
- **Olive Omnipotent**
- **Dr. Green (psychiatrist)**
- **Dr. Joints (physician)**
- **Dr. Inhale (dentist)**
- **Jason David (Body Guard #1)**
- **Stan Hudson (Body Guard #2)**
- **Chris Baker (Body Guard #3)**
- **Jason Cox**
- **Joshua Hudson-Omnipotent**
- **Craig Porter**
- **John Derringer**
- **Kim Mitchell**
- **Andy Frost**
- **Al Joynes**
- **John Scholes**
- **Alice Copper**
- **Jeff Woods**
- **Little Stevens**
- **Ryan Parker**
- **Frank Stronach**
- **Victor White**
- **Tommy Davis**
- **William Shatter**
- **Wayne Gretzky**
- **Mick Jaggar**
- **Wayne Brady**
- **Jimmy Carson**
- **Jimmy Page**
- **Robert Plant**

- **Ozzy Osbourne**
- **Tom Cruise**
- **Tom Hanks**
- **Sean Connery**
- **Shawn Henry**
- **Reginald Jackson**
- **Mel Gibson**
- **Sylvester Stallone**
- **Arnold Schwarzenegger**
- **Chris Rock**
- **Thomas Omnipotent**
- **Marshall Mathers III**
- **Aubrey Graham**
- **Ray Edwards**
- **Nigel Leaf**
- **Charles Dean**
- **Adrian Mosley**
- **Daniel John**
- **Dale Chris**
- **William Roberts**
- **Dustin Flames**
- **Arnold James**
- **Kelly Riley**
- **Brian Wade**
- **Ben Glass**
- **Sidney Crosby**
- **Don Cherry**
- **Jackie Chan**
- **Phillip McGraw**
- **Eddie Murphy**
- **Eddie Bauer**
- **Bruno Mars**
- **Monica Wade (lawyer)**
- **Jennifer Wesley (case manager)**
- **Dorothy Omnipotent-Page**
- **Joanne Wilder**
- **Maureen Holloway**
- **Shakira Ripoll**

- Jennifer Aniston
- Jennifer Lopez
- Cindy Crawford
- Cindy Margolis
- Samantha Fox
- Tracy Chapman
- Ricki Lake
- Nicki Minaj
- Belinda Stronach
- Robyn Fenty
- Adele Adkins
- Dana Anderson
- Katrina Carter
- Jean Potter
- Yuki Villegas
- Cindy Summers
- Alyssa Milano
- Kristian Alfonso
- Orpah Winfrey
- Martina Hingis
- Marry Bloom-Ching
- Nicole Kidman
- Drew Barrymore
- Sandra Bullock
- Janet Jackson
- Janet Gretzky
- Susan Sarandon
- Susan Summers
- Kim Kardashian
- Britney Spears
- Rachelle Smith
- Hannah Omnipotent-Baker

*Silver Cards go to:*

**Sarah Omnipotent-Hudson**
**Ashley Omnipotent-Hudson**
**James Johnson**

*Bronze Card Go To:*

- **Mexico Citizens generation after generation**
- **David Hudson (if you can get $10,000 Canadian Cash in a bank account receive a Gold Card)(work hard and go get your dreams)**

*Pink Cards Go To:*

- **American Citizens generation after generation**

*Names on list of cards and new cards,* **CAN NOT BE TAKEN OFF!!** **(I pray I spelt everyone's name right, I apologize if I didn't no disrespect)**

**Money Card Rules:**

*Platinum Card* **= Freedom**
(Only bring what you need)
(Total assets in a country is $100,000,000 *Canadian Cash* over life time ban)
(Must have $100,000 *Canadian Cash* in a bank account in that country no less or lifetime ban)

**Emotion cards**

**Green Cards**:
You are NCR *(Not Criminally Responsible)* and your keeping a secret and reality has made you a walking zombie!!!

*Rules of the* **Green Card**:

Must take the secret/secrets to your grave! Post one on the back of the stone!!!

## Money Cards

- ***Platinum Card***
$1,000,000,000,000
*Canadian Cash*
- ***Gold Card***
$1,000,000,000
*Canadian Cash*
- **Silver Card**
$1,000,000
*Canadian Cash*
- **Bronze Card**
$1,000
*Canadian Cash*

**Pink Card**
$1
*Canadian Cash*

## Book
*Green 24*

## Chapter
*Monopoly*

- Platinum Card (you own the world you can do whatever the fuck you want with-in reason) if you can prove your blood family, if you're not on the cards list (receive a **Silver Card**)!! You will be taken care of before and after cremation with a card if you're still alive!!!! Promotions are available!! ***Gold card*** maximum!! (Auditors are everywhere)!!!

**Book**
*-777, Insomnia*

**Chapter**
*177777771, Movie*

Whoever plays me in a movie, receive two **Gold Cards**. If we die and there's a movie made out of hear say about me!!!! Those Actors will receive a **Platinum Card**!!

**Book**
*0, A New Way Of Life*

**Chapter**
*O, The Newest Period*
*So when....*

*To Be Continued...*

**Book**
*Incarnated*

**Chapter**
*-47*

If you knew where you are going, how would you change your life?

*More to come...*

**Book**
*The Fountain Of Souls*

**Chapter**
*A New Emotion*

There's nothing like a woman's smile. We are losing Mother Earth. Please, Please, Smile. The **Heavens** will open. Give her peace back!!

Imagination is what got us here in the first place. We have never lost it!!

Wherever the energy of life may travel, "mine will connect with yours". When it connects a new creation will mature thought-out and before/after these Universes with Dimensions and even beyond the limits of space & time...

Wanting and waiting for your soul to be released into the Unknowing. What's it called? You know after before black matter. There's something else out there.... If there isn't, than don't let us dream it!!

Out of all of our dads sperm We were given life and thank **God** for that egg!! Team work!!.. Mother Father (The World), King Queen, Oil Water.. We need to be two!! We are losing Mother Earth our answers to eternal life step two!! The mind (soul) it's endless like the Internet, the black hole of life!!

**Book**
*Jukebox*

**Chapter**
*7, Reincarnation (The Stairway To **Heaven**)(Led Zeppelin)*

*(Yeah right roflmfao)*

Humans, animals, fish, insects! We all have the same rights. We are in for a rude awakening. Whatever makes you happy while you're on earth (so its whatever) there are no borders in hell or temples. All for one, one looking for two. If you really what to be an animal, insect or fish, find your better half in **Hell**. Make it to heaven together. Everything is controlled on earth. Remember we can only produce life with the same species... C'mon people wake-up. So why consume so much flesh and animal milk. We don't need our wisdom teeth and formula and soy milk is better for us (manmade!!)

**Book**
*Nest*

**Chapter**
*Smack in the middle, **Purgatory***

1- If you die before your husband or wife you go to **Purgatory** (the nest of waiting souls) you wait until your children are married and for your other half, if they die, for the next step?

2- If you don't get married you go to **Hell** to find a soul to break free (find a miscarriage or abortion) the more you know the more valuable you are!! Let's get educated!

3- If you have an abortion (Murder)(Death Penalty is also murder) you go to **Hell** (to serve your time) with the spouse separated (if you find your abortion or one of them, straight to **Heaven** for the Solemnities of Soul Mating, child climbs, *The Stairway To Heaven,* where they start? The older the higher and that child is on its way to **Heaven**.... (2 late it's gone) it's a hell of a lot easier to go your separate ways in **Hell** but if you find each other!! Then what's after **Heaven!!!!**

4- The only way to get a divorced is through an abortion (if you're married and have a child by another person and get an abortion) you and your other half have sacrificed your child and ex-spouse to **Hell**, be happy you're on your way to **Heaven** with a fresh start....

5- If your soul isn't taken from **Purgatory** you go to **Hell** after the Solemnities of Soul Mating.

6- If your child or one of your children die before they get married, you both go to **Hell**

(Some souls want to stay but they can't we have to free **Purgatory** then **Hell** is Next!)

**Book**
*Three*

**Chapter**
*5, The First Fertilization*

*Have You Heard Of Purgatory?*

Not every Mother or Father gets a pass into ***Heaven*** (not with this society) we have to make sacrifices. We are human, we have to provide life, to reach the next step!! Only the first growth in the womb, will determine your fate.

*Our family Tree*

Female ***Goddess*** (together forever) Male ***God*** = child *(**life**)*

Men can bear as many children with as many virgin wombs on earth as long as he has the first growth, this includes miscarriages and abortions.

　　This will determine his fate in *purgatory*. The first child will connect the souls to get to the next step!! Choose one! we are losing the women's soul in purgatory...

　　I don't want some other man growing life in my home the womb ifs it's pure with my Fathers life!! if its mine too. It's incest (the deadly sin and only sin)!!!

　　There are ways around everything, (must give birth to a child and marry them).

　　Okay so there's Fantasy and Reality put Together = *Society*.

　　So we can predict our future!! Why?

　　What if the appendix was the holding sac for sperm? Let say we have a pure son/daughter, lets look at this in a spiritual way (We don't know before or after the first child's growth.. yet!!) say a woman gives a man a blow job and swallows once, otherwise it's incest cant mix... Pure.. Just in case!!

　　It's only in the natural equations of love, that any reasonable reason can be found. Everybody is the reason we are, we all are the reasons we are. Our minds processes so fast (John Nash, R.I.P. you died with your wife, be with her forever), We can keep up with it. The papers are in the right files upstairs. Jumping from one thing to the other the web of life. There is so much out there. The answer are here on earth!! The beginnings are here with no end!!

*We have not lost our grip on reality*
*We know what's real and what's in our mind*
*We can rest in peace*
*We will make a difference in* **Heaven** *or* **Hell**
*The more we know the more valuable we are!!*
*Amen!!*

**Book**
*Mirror*

**Chapter**
*458, AQU Eye Contact*

Make eye contact with everything, learn the soul, feel the soul. Blink, dream the soul!

**Book**
*Two Of A Kind*

**Chapter**
*Three, Educating the mind and soul*

What if your abortion or miscarriage or child had the cure for HIV or cancer in their soul . (Or even a masturbation) at the same point masturbation got us here, it's life! From the soil (insects) I am not an animal, fish, insect. I can kill them and eat them!!! I'm a Homo Sapien! With **Celestial** Homo Sapiens!!

**Book**
*96, The Pill, Miscarriages, Abortions*

**Chapter**
*Two, I don't know*

I lied to everyone trying to protect my sons mother. We were breaking my bail conditions. I also thought WE were pregnant (January 2009) before the NCR assessment. I should have the right to know if my son's mother had an abortion, or if it was a miscarriage of false birth. I found literature in our old bedroom about abortions. Why do women have all the rights? I would have asked her to take care of the child until she gives birth then let me raise the child if we can't do it as a team!! I would have asked because she has all the rights in **Canada!**

To be continued!!

**Book**
*69*

**Chapter**
*% Holy Grail*

Marijuana = *Mary You Wanna?*

Not every son wants to sleep with their mother....

**Book**
*Food & Water*

**Chapter**
*The Choice*

Everything is food and water, if it isn't we digest it, don't over use your asshole! Shower after you shit, wash away what the body doesn't need. We use moistened cloths for babies and White Petroleum Jelly. When I give oral sex, I clean my lady sucking and swallowing the food. Then we suck each other's mouth, swapping and giving her energy and food (then it's my turn to reach ecstasy).... **My lady** always cums first!! Playing Dracula is yummy (I'd rather eat my wife's blood before Bambi's)

## Book
*Daily Ritual*

## Chapter
*Bionic*

*Wake-up, morning, around 6:00am*

- Test ph in urine
- One joint of weed ($5.00)
- One stick of cigarette ($0.30 cents)
- ph strip ($0.13 cents)

Two lemons freshly squeezed with 600ml of water, drink with one multi-vitamin and mineral, one calcium and magnesium pill, one vitamin E pill and one acetylsalicylic acid tablet (aspirin).

- Lemon ($0.50 cents) x 2
- Multi-Vitamin and Mineral ($0.15 cents)
- Calcium and Magnesium pill ($0.10 cents)
- Vitamin E pill (($0.10 cents)
- Aspirin ($0.02)
- Bottle of water ($0.20 cents) x 2

Drink right before 5km run with push-ups and sit-ups.....

After run around 7:30am

300ml of freshly squeezed grapefruit, then prepare shake 15 minutes later, drink shake right away.

- grapefruit ($1.50) x 1.5

**SHAKE**
- 2 egg whites ($0.35 cents) x 2
- 1 ½ cups of soy milk ($0.50 cents)
- 1 banana ($0.75 cents)
- 3 strawberries ($0.10 cents) x 3

**AFTER SHAKE**
- Coffee ($0.40 cents)

*9:00am*

Test ph levels in urine and balance
Just a guide if ph is around 6.0 this combination brings ph to 7.5 plus.....

One teaspoon of baking soda with 3 teaspoons of freshly squeezed lemon, combine ingredients and let fizz, then add 400ml of water and 2 tablespoons of un-pasteurized honey and drink....

- Baking soda ($0.01 cents)
- Lemon ($0.13 cents)
- ph strip ($0.13 cents)
- Bottle of water ($0.20 cents)
- Unpasteurized honey, ($0.50 cents) x 2

*10:30am*

350ml of vegetable juice ($1.50)

*Noon 12:00pm (lunch)*

Test ph urine levels and adjust, drink 250ml of prune juice with lunch (no meat) after lunch one joint of weed and one stick of cigarette.

- Prune juice ($1.50)
- One joint of weed ($5.00)
- One stick of cigarette ($0.30)
- Lunch ($8.00)
- ph strip ($0.13 cents)

2:00pm

-   500ml Chocolate Milk ($1.50)

*4:00pm to 9:00pm*

Test ph in urine around 4:00pm

-   3 tall cans of Miller Genuine Draft Beer
-   2 joints of weed
-   2 sticks of cigarette
-   bottle of water ($0.20 cents) x 2

Dinner meat included (chicken, beef, pork and fish) with a glass of red wine

-   2 joints of weed ($5.00) x 2
-   2 sticks of cigarette ($0.30 cents)
-   3 tall cans of beer ($2.40) x 3
-   1 glass of red wine ($3.00)
-   Dinner ($15.00)
-   ph strip ($0.13 cents)

*Before bed*

Test ph in urine and balance

300ml of cranberry juice and then detox tea before bed.

-   Cranberry juice ($1.50)
-   Tea ($0.60 cents)
-   50ml of Seroquel (free)
-   Baking soda ($0.01 cents)
-   Lemon ($0.13 cents)
-   ph strip ($0.13 cents)

My daily ritual happens almost every day of the year, I haven't figured out my calendar year yet, there will be some fasting days and special meal days. My daily ritual is divided into two categories, Internal and External.... Internal comes out my ass and penis, skin. Taste, nails, shit like that and External is the air and the smoke we breathe, vapours, steam, smell shit like that. With Marijuana comes Tobacco, Weed = Life, Smokes = Death..... with food comes ph balancing, Food & Water = Life, over/under 7.7 = a miserable death.....

-Weed and cigarettes = ($21.20) a day, a month = ($636)
-Food and ph strips = ($51.40) a day, a month = (($1,542)

**Total**
= a day ($72.60)
=a month ($2,178)

Please Help Me!! I need royalties and medical marijuana and food allowance in Canada, Canada's life expectancy is around 85, I want to live past that, forever young. I've smoked pot and cigarettes and drank alcohol my whole life and I'm not about to quit, I've gotten this far and I want to get further with my strict calendar year. I have my own religion and I will go the distance with My Angel, I have Books and Chapters to prove it. Please Help Me get my life dreams of peace and the enjoyment of life in my brain...... Injection once a month and let My Angel and I be free. I don't have Schizophrenia, God gave me everything, now I'm giving it all to My Angel and she's the biggest giver in all the Universes with Dimensions. I'm in a true love story!!

-Cook meat separate (including soup)

**Book**
*$ Job*

**Chapter**
*Resume*

**Olive Omnipotent**
*69 Heaven Way*
*Suit #7*
*Weedville, Hidden Valley, Faraway*

*G3T G0D*
*112-224-6942*
*Justcallmegod@hi5.fa*

*Highlights Of Qualification*

- Over 20years customer service Experience
- Excellent work record; proven ability to achieve promotions
- Dedicated employee; able to work well in a team or independently
- Self motivator who is dedicated to their tasks and ensure they are completed with high quality and creativeness
- Strong multi-tasking individual who has the ability to remain calm in stressful situations
- Good problem solver with strong organizational skills
- Has experience in several different career fields and I have a wide range of diverse opinions
- Maintains professional relationships by presenting a friendly and positive attitude

*Work Industry Experience*

- Over 2 years in the Canadian Military as an Infantry Soldier; two years of hard work and discipline
- I take pride in maintaining a clean and safe work environment
- Communicates well with customers and ensures that their exceptions are met and exceeded
- Knowledge of chemical and physical adjustments to keep painting products and procedures within guideline specifications
- Experience with a large variety of food preparation ranging from pasta dishes to breakfast cuisines
- Experience with heavy machine operation including Grinders, Punch Presses and CNC Machines
- Skilled and experience including, but not limited to: assembling, analyzing, exploring, opening and finishing
- Turned a 200 paper route into a 500 paper route
- I take pleasure in working, the more we know the more valuable we are

*Other Employment Experience*

*Gods Heatreat Ltd.*
Paint Mixer 1995-1999
*Canadian Forces*
Infantry Soldier 1998-2001
*The Faraway Post*
Self Employed – Courier Service 2001-2006
*Trailer's To Heaven*
Order Picker 2001-2003
 *Aerospace Machinists*
Maintenance 2003-2004
*Magnets Poles*
Tool and Die (assistant) 2005-2006
*Contractors/Home Renovation*
Construction Laborer 2006-2008
*Unemployed And Homeless*
Employment insurance/ Ontario Works/ODSP 2009-2011
*Hockey Donuts*
Baker 2011-2014
*Education*

*First Aid and CPR Training 1997/2003*
*WHMIS Training 1997/2003*
*Ontario Secondary School Diploma 1998*
*Precision Machining & Tooling 2004*
*Basic and advance Chef 2009*
*Forklift Operator Certification Expiry-06/12/2015*

**Happy Birthday To Creation**

*July 02/2013(Hail **Mary**)*

This Book was Created because of Woman and Men and Animals and Everything, with special thanks to **Honey Celestial Bloom!! Our Angel!!** With love in all ways....

*Made with my iPhone 4S 64GB*
*Edited with Microsoft Word 2007*

Manufactured by Amazon.ca
Acheson, AB

15289383R00104